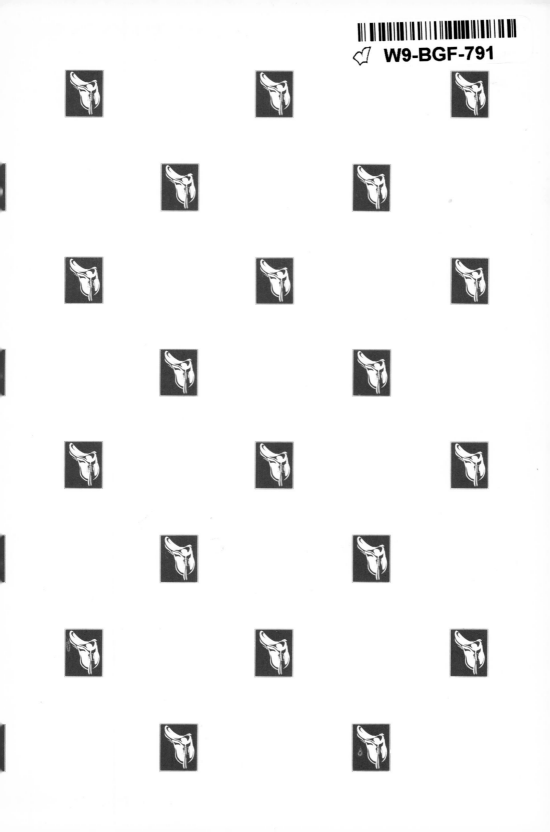

▪ THE JOCKEY CLUB COOKBOOK ▪

THE
▪ JOCKEY CLUB ▪

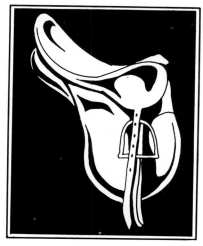

▪ COOKBOOK ▪

BY STAN DWORKIN

*Photographs by William Pell
and Aldo Tutino*

TAYLOR PUBLISHING COMPANY
Dallas, Texas

Copyright © 1985, Taylor Publishing Company
All rights reserved.
No part of this publication may be reproduced in any
form, or by any means, without permission in
writing from the publisher.

Illustration and Book Design by Tina K. Forster

Dust jacket photograph of the author
by Warren Inglese

Food Styling by Betty Pell

Library of Congress Cataloging in Publication Data
Dworkin, Stan.
    The Jockey Club Cookbook.

    Includes index.

    1. Cookery. 2. Jockey Club Restaurant (New York,
N.Y.) 3. New York (N.Y.) — Restaurants. 4. Jockey
Club Restaurant (Washington, D.C.) 5. Washington,
D.C. — Restaurants. I. Title.
TX715.D9735 1985   641.5'09747'1   84-16155
ISBN 0-87833-453-X

Printed in the United States of America

First edition. 9 8 7 6 5 4 3 2 1

RF/KF

To my wife,
my partner, my lover, and my friend—
who all just happen to be the same person:
Floss Romm Dworkin

▪ CONTENTS ▪

LIST OF COLOR PLATES

▪ PART ONE ▪

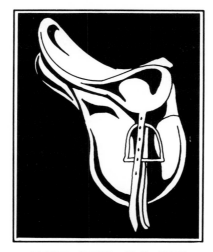

▪ UP FRONT ▪

Acknowledgments
Preface
Upstairs/Downstairs
Glossary

▪ ACKNOWLEDGMENTS ▪

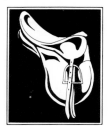

I want to thank a lot of people for their participation in the making of *The Jockey Club Cookbook:*

First of all, Executive Chef Daniel Dunas, Executive Chef Marcel Van Eeckhaut, Sous-Chefs David Biela, Alain de Coster, Tom Kelman, and Richard Mikolitch, Pastry Chef Danny Michel, and Pastry Cook Danny Beeckmans—all of whom, to various degrees, shared with me their recipes, techniques, and experiences, and sometimes their friendship.

Maître d'Hôtel Martin Garbisu and Assistant Maître d' Gilbert Jean, of the D.C. Jockey Club, for their good humor and assistance, and Maître d'Hôtel Marcel Eusebi of the New York Jockey Club for his help. Sommelier John Benevento of the New York Jockey Club and Beverage Director Bill Kennedy of the D.C. Jockey Club for their wine suggestions.

Next, Frank Bowling (managing director of the New York Ritz-Carlton) and Eric Ewoldt (vice-president and managing director of the Washington, D.C., Ritz-Carlton) and Jan Morton (special assistant in the executive office in D.C.) for their unfailing courtesy and accommodation.

Finally, John B. Coleman, owner of the two Jockey Clubs, who opened all doors for me and made this book possible. I asked him once if he had a philosophy about the Jockey Clubs, and he answered without hesitation: "A hotel restaurant does not have to look like a hotel restaurant."

When you walk into either of the Jockey Clubs, you'd have to say that he is a man who has implemented his philosophy.

▪ PREFACE ▪

The recipes in *The Jockey Club Cookbook* come from two of the great kitchens in this country. That they are both named the Jockey Club Restaurant is no coincidence. It's rather a testimony to the willingness of John B. Coleman, the owner of the Ritz-Carlton hotels in New York City and Washington, D.C., and the two Jockey Club restaurants attached to them, to do what had to be done to make them great.

These are not recipes from books, they are recipes from cooks.

They are the recipes of the dishes served on a day-to-day basis in these great kitchens.

They are recipes from men whose lives have been the kitchen— mature men dedicated to the re-creation and the remolding of the classical and young men dedicated to the creation of the new.

These are men who are as much artists in their white coats and *toques* as painters are in their smocks. And if you had been with me, looking over their shoulders as they created, you'd have no doubt about it.

The leading characters in this book—Chef Daniel Dunas of New York and Chef Marcel Van Eeckhaut of Washington, D.C.—have been in kitchens from the ages of fourteen and sixteen. I was not raised to the world of cooking. I have been a cook for only twenty-two years. I have written cookbooks of original recipes and taught bread-baking with my wife, Floss, but that doesn't compare to a lifetime of dedication to cuisine.

However, the years I have spent in my own kitchens, cooking and creating recipes for my other cookbooks, do give me something. They give me the ability to talk "kitchen"; the ability to understand (if only after repeated explanations) the difference between *bain-marie* and *beurre manié*; the ability to *translate*.

I don't just mean translate from French to English. (Yes, there was a good deal of French to translate, but I used to speak French, and it comes back—and there are dictionaries.) I translated from metric measurements to U.S.; from pounds to cups; and from "handfuls" and "serving-spoons" to more conventional measures. And, finally, I tried to translate from restaurant kitchen to home kitchen; I tried to adapt the recipes, without changing them.

Sometimes, when the ingredients in a recipe were for more servings than I felt you could readily prepare in one batch at home, I reduced the amounts before I tested them in my kitchen.

These recipes came together by a combination of routes. Some of them were handwritten by the chefs (or typed by a typist from handwriting) and given to me to reproduce. When I was given the chefs' work in this form, I sat down with them and went over the steps. Then I tested the recipes, wrote them up, and gave them again to the chefs (or pastry chef or sous-chef) to check.

Most of the recipes were dictated to me from memory by the chefs and cooks. (I think these were my favorite times: sitting and sipping —wine, or beer, or sometimes champagne—writing down techniques and recipes from these talented men.) I tested them, worked them into legible form, and gave them back to the chefs to double-check.

And some few were taken from the chefs' old notes. In some respects, these were the toughest to deal with. For sometimes the notes were quite a distance from the way the recipe was actually being prepared in the restaurants, and my goal was to present the dishes as they were and are being prepared.

Then, there was the necessity to try the dishes. After all, I had to know how they tasted to be certain I had reproduced them accurately, didn't I? I had to sit down and eat excellent meal after excellent meal in these fine restaurants, submitting to the perfect service. As the saying goes: It was a dirty job, but someone had to do it.

I must add here that I was surprised at the total cooperation these two kitchens gave me. I was warned that most chefs are quite jealous of their secrets, and will often leave out a crucial ingredient. It didn't happen here.

There were accidents and typing errors. The recipe for Rice Pudding (page 188) was originally sent to me without the rice listed; Scallops and Turbot Mousse (page 111) had no cooking instructions— without which it is a lot of raw fish. But when I pointed out the lack, we shared a laugh, and there was never a hesitation to give me the correct instructions.

There is no way to describe the excitement I felt as the beauty and logic of the recipes unfolded before me. Sometimes I felt myself to be a detective, searching for the one flaw (that one bit of information left out of a description) that kept a recipe from working. Sometimes I felt like an analyst, trying to draw out a hidden piece of the past. Sometimes I felt like an acolyte being instructed in something close to the religious mysteries. Sometimes, when a recipe just worked so slick and smooth, I felt like a direct descendant of Escoffier. But always, I felt the thrill of the chase. After all, these *are* the recipes of the Jockey Club.

How to Use This Book

If you have some experience as a cook, you should have no difficulty with these recipes at all. My wife says that they should present little problem to anyone who can cook a decent breakfast. If you've had very little experience in cooking, but would still like to try one of these gems for a dinner party, or even just for yourself (there are many recipes for one or two), then I suggest two things: Glance through the Glossary before you start to read the recipes, and read through the whole recipe before you begin to cook.

There is a great deal of explanatory information in the Glossary. Don't feel you have to memorize it before you can start cooking. The Glossary is a reference section, intended to explain terms, ingredients, processes—*as I use them in this book, and as I understand them to be used in the Jockey Club kitchens.*

Whether you are experienced or not, if you come across an unfamiliar term, or phrase, or a process that you feel is not fully explained, try the Glossary. Sometimes it is difficult to take the time within a recipe to fully explain a subsidiary process. I have taken that time in the Glossary.

All these recipes are *possible!* Some of them are complicated—as only classical French cuisine can be complicated. Others are so simple and quick that you'll have trouble believing they can be as good as they are.

Whether your own tastes run to the simple or the complex, I hope you will get as much pleasure from these recipes as I did.

Bon appétit!

Wines

I am by no stretch of the imagination (yours or mine) a wine expert.

The only wines I know beyond a bare nodding acquaintance (I nod at the bottles as I pass them on the rack) are the white Burgundies of the Route de Grands Crus and the Mosels of Luxembourg and Alsace, and those because of a trip made from *cave* to *cave* about ten years ago. Which means my information is ten years out of date.

So, if it were up to me, I would probably recommend Meursault with everything.

Fortunately, it is not up to me. Fortunately, I have experts to call on for wine recommendations.

In New York, the wines were suggested by Sommelier John Benevento, a man with many years' experience in wine for fine food.

In Washington, D.C., the wines were suggested by Beverage Manager Bill Kennedy, and by Executive Chef Marcel Van Eeckhaut.

Where possible, the suggestions are taken from the Jockey Clubs' own wine lists. (The two restaurants have completely different wine lists and different wine-buying practices.) Otherwise, more generic suggestions have been made.

Where my experts felt that they could not suggest a particular wine for a particular dish, they passed.

Or, as one of them said when confronted by a particularly spicy recipe, "I think I'd rather have a German beer with this."

▪ UPSTAIRS/DOWNSTAIRS ▪

If you have dined or lunched at either of the Jockey Club restaurants—in New York or D.C.—you know what it's like, and you are reading *The Jockey Club Cookbook* to find out how they do it. For you, this section may be somewhat redundant. You may want to skip on to the descriptions of the kitchens or even to the recipes themselves.

However, if your experience with the Jockey Clubs is a newspaper review or a photo in a magazine, then let me introduce you on a more personal level.

Washington, D.C.

In the District of Columbia, the entrance to the Ritz-Carlton is at the corner of Massachusetts Avenue NW and 21st Street—right on the corner, at an angle to the street. The driveway that cuts across the corner is bricked and cobblestoned, and the glass and brass doors are tall, but not as wide as most hotel entrances.

The Ritz-Carlton's lobby consists of white marble tile and blue-gray-painted wood, and is small for the lobby of a hotel of international reputation. But then this is a small hotel. It prides itself not on the number of guests it can serve, but on the services it can deliver to its guests.

The concierge is stationed on the left side of the lobby, the reception desk takes up a good portion of the right side.

A half-dozen steps past the entrance will take you to the lobby-wide marble stairs. Walk straight ahead, and you'll find yourself in front of the elevators; bear to the left a bit, and you'll see the Fairfax Bar; farther to the left is the entrance to the Jockey Club.

If it is dinnertime, then Martin's handsome face will greet you. Regulars get big hellos, but everyone gets a smile. Martin is a Basque, and the only Basque I've ever met; I can't tell if his accent is typical. If Martin is a typical Basque, then the Basques must be the most charming people on Earth. If it is lunchtime or Saturday, then you may be greeted by Gilbert, easily identified by his Southern accent—the south of France, that is.

The restaurant is mostly of dark wood, with a couple of light-stucco walls. The ceilings are beamed and cross-boarded with the same dark wood, across panels that give the look of that same stucco. Perhaps as many as fifty cylindrical yellow lanterns cast a gentle light. This is a restaurant that looks to have been in the same place for a long time—which indeed it has. Many of the wood carvings look Oriental, others European. The paintings and prints carry out the Jockey Club motif: hunt and racing images. Some of the statuary is most handsome. In fact, there is on the bar a small bronze of three pigs that I would love to see on my own mantle.

A visitor standing in the entryway can see down through most of the restaurant—though those sitting at some of the tables would be hidden by the waist-high banquettes.

What is the best table in the house? It's really the clientele that decides that. Those tables most asked for are the "best," and different regulars have different preferences. For a while, when one member of a VIF (Very Important Family) took the same corner table every time she came in, then that corner was the "best" and the most desirable. Even those tables farthest back and farthest away are desirable for those who want that fabled "quiet table in the corner." The banquettes are comfortable, the tables and chairs are just tables and chairs. The table linen is cream colored with a red pattern (red overplaid, bordered by a red bunch of grapes and grape leaves).

The D.C. Jockey Club is not a spectacularly fancy restaurant, but it is a spectacularly comfortable one—at least everyone and everything combine to make a diner *feel* comfortable—and, yes, like a member of the club.

The service is vigorously elegant. The captains and waiters are all pros, with centuries of experience among them. Do you want something not on the menu? Do you want something that was on the menu last week? Ask your captain.

The last time I dined at the D.C. Jockey Club, a French couple sat at the next table. In the District Jockey Club, the tables are surprisingly close together (I say "surprisingly" because there is a great deal of business talked at the D.C. tables, especially during lunch—and yet, as close as they are, the business does get talked). During their discussion of dinner, being the kind of person I am, I recommended to them the Gâteau Marjolaine (recipe on page 200), which was on the pastry cart that evening.

They smiled and nodded at the suggestion, and we both went about eating our dinners. I did not have Gâteau Marjolaine that evening; I had Strawberries Romanoff (recipe on page 191), a dish I needed to taste before I prepared it at home.

Well, the couple noted that I was not following my own recommendation and asked me why, and we got into a good deal more conversation.

They were French, but residing now in Montreal, and great travelers. And as they traveled, their hobby was . . . food.

Through the rest of their meal, they commented to me about the quality of the dishes, and how well they compared to the very best they had tasted anywhere.

Being in our nation's capital, the Jockey Club is frequented by travelers from all over the world, by the highest of high society, by senators and congressmen, by ambassadors and diplomats, and even presidents. How does the food compare? Well, they keep coming back.

New York City

In New York, the Ritz-Carlton Hotel is on Central Park South, between Seventh Avenue and Avenue of the Americas, its blue and white canopies almost inconspicuous among several others belonging to hotels with higher profiles.

While there is an entrance within the hotel, the main entrance to the Jockey Club is from the street. One passes through a tiny entryway, then into a clublike alcove—with tables, banquettes, padded chairs, and bookcases full of books—as annex to the bar. One day I saw Melina Mercouri holding court here, surrounded by Greek-language newspapers and Greek-language speakers—and coffee and desserts.

From this alcove, one descends a few wooden stairs to the bar. Just past the end of the bar is the maître d's desk; just past that is the entrance to the restaurant itself.

In New York, the maîtres d'hôtel are tuxedoed, lunch and dinner. There is no casualness here. The New York Jockey Club is seriously posh.

The restaurant's rooms and the bar and its alcove are all paneled in glossy antique pine. The paneling is all but covered with antique hunting prints and paintings of animals—many of them nineteenth century English works.

There are three rooms in the restaurant. The first is almost a wide hallway, which holds the permanent dessert table in its center, and tables for diners down its sides. It is here that the famous often request to be seated to be seen and to see. The central room is the main room. It has a fireplace at one end, and it is the first room to fill when the restaurant is crowded. The last room is my favorite. By some it is considered Coventry because it holds the kitchen entrance, but it, too, has a fireplace, and a quiet and secluded feeling.

The chairs are high-backed and leather-padded; the banquettes are of leather too. The china is beautiful Spode, and the peach-colored table linens are almost heavy enough to build houses from.

Elegant—truly elegant. Here the conversation is more muted. Even at lunchtime, the pace is slower. Business lunches in the New York Jockey Club tend to be two- (or three-) hour affairs.

But the elegance is not intimidating. Rather, it is a comfortable elegance, with the waiters and captains helpful and attentive (but not hovering so as to be annoying).

Like the D.C. Jockey Club, the air is, indeed, like that of a club—a more luxurious club, a quieter club, but, for all that, a comfortable club.

The Kitchens

It's a little like being in a tropical storm—the heat, the rush of activity. The main difference is that in a storm there is none of the purposefulness that surrounds you in a kitchen, and, of course, the storm doesn't hit the same place twice a day.

I have spent hours in both kitchens, watching lunches and dinners being prepared and plated for service—and even practicing some of the skills I needed to prepare the recipes in this book. It was an exciting time.

The D.C. Kitchen

The D.C. kitchen is laid out like an old railroad flat (am I showing my age?): Everything is pretty much visible in one straight line a few steps after you enter.

Right inside the door is the salad kitchen. This is separate from the main stoves, to prevent the salad ingredients from wilting in the heat. Two women at a time make the salads. They work only on salads (and cold breakfast dishes), and they are the only women in the kitchen.

Next in is the pastry kitchen, with its own oven and a marble-topped preparation table. Marble is great for working pastry. Pastry requires some degree of coolness (on the part of both the pastry chef and the ingredients)—at least when making actual pastry—but there is very little coolness here in the summer and spring months. Pastry Chef Danny Michel told me about the summer he went about rolling pastry by laying ice on his marble surface for 20 minutes, and then drying it and rolling dough for 20 minutes, and then icing again.

That's a tough way to beat the heat. When the new kitchen is completed, it will have facilities for cooling the pastry kitchen.

There is a space of a few feet between the pastry oven and the bouillon cauldron, past which the main bank of stoves begins.

At the corner is the *saucier*'s station. In the D.C. Jockey Club the *saucier* not only makes sauces, he may also make stocks during the day and prepare some of the main courses at night.

The next station is the *poissonier*'s, the fish chef's. In many restaurants, this is a minor post, but at dinnertime in D.C., fish is a very popular dish, and this post really hops. This is where the heat begins to get fierce. The *saucier* can step back, away from the ovens, into the space between his post and the pastry kitchen, but not the *poissonier*. In addition to waist-high stove-ovens, both of these stations have overhead salamanders for glazing and quick reheating.

Past the *poissonier* is the meat chef's station, with its stove and broiler, and the vegetable chef's, with its deep-fat fryer.

Past the stoves is the back exit to the outside world—a door that seems to be always open, to provide a bit of fresh air—and past the door, inside, additional preparation space. In this area, one can often find Chef Marcel Van Eeckhaut preparing special dishes for banquets.

Behind the chefs, as they face their heat-blackened stoves, running from the *saucier*'s to the vegetable man's positions, is the stainless steel plating table. This is a two-tier table, and for its entire length, the top level serves as a platform to hold various pots, pans, and serving dishes. (Continuously, through the mealtime, these metal and crockery pieces are washed by the dishwasher and repiled on that upper surface.) At the end in back of the *saucier*, the lower level is a large hot-water bath that serves as a *bain-marie* and holds sauces and stocks that must be kept warm. Down the rest of the kitchen, the lower level serves as a plating surface (that area where the cooks actually put the cooked food on dishes), and as an interface for the waiters.

It is behind this counter that the waiters wait, and where they, in D.C., put the garnishes, sauces, and final touches to the dishes before serving. (In New York, the chefs do most of these finishing touches themselves.)

It is in this waiters' area that the sous-chef is stationed. If the moment is quiet, he may be doing some chore. One evening, Sous-Chef Tom Kelman was working on Quenelles of Salmon (recipe on page 105) in quiet moments; another evening, Sous-Chef Dave Biela was cutting potatoes into the appropriate shape for Pommes Soufflés (recipe on page 55).

In D.C. they use a computer system. The waiter comes inside the kitchen and, just inside the door, types his orders (table number, items ordered) into the computer; a small printout pops out of a related machine at the sous-chef's station; the sous-chef picks it up, calls out the appropriate orders to the appropriate cooks, and puts the slip of paper onto a hook numbered with the table number.

As things busy up, the sous-chef marches up and down, keeping an eye on what's what: Is this dish cooking too dry? Is that plating too wet? Are we running short of Crab Cakes (recipe on page 109)?·

If a special dish is wanted for a VIP—something not on the menu, or not on the menu that night—it is to the ranking chef that the enquiring captain (or Maître d'Hôtel Martin himself, if the personage is important enough) comes. He asks the ranking chef, and the request will be filled—or not. Chefs are very independent folks, folks.

The kitchen is not a noisy place by industrial standards, but it is noisy enough: the clatter of the pots and dishes, the orders, the waiters' inquiries (food seldom comes out fast enough for the waiters), the conversation (during meals, this is not so much conversation as it is banter—the working kitchen is no place to carry on a considered conversation).

There is an advertisement currently on TV purporting to show a kitchen in a cooking school, with chefs preparing various exotic dishes as you watch. The pace is regal, the white uniforms are spotless, and the air tranquil. Very attractive, but as a picture of a functioning kitchen, the only connection it has to reality is the food.

The whites that start out so clean every morning are quickly spotted and stained as first raw and then cooked foods are handled; the pace is frantic; and the air is charged with the pressure of a half-dozen men preparing perhaps 250 dishes within the space of a few hours. And preparing them so that they have the special look—and taste—that marks a first-class kitchen.

The New York Kitchen

The New York Jockey Club kitchen looks quite different. The first difference is the view right past the swinging door. In Washington, a few steps in and you can see the entire row of cooks; you can turn to the left and see the salad kitchen, which doubles as the room-service kitchen and triples as the cold-breakfast kitchen, but you can see very little of the cooking areas themselves.

In New York, the cooking areas are wings that give off a main corridor down one side of the kitchen. All these wings are dead-ended, which means that all cooks enter and leave by the same side. Not much of an inconvenience unless you have to carry a sack of potatoes past two other cooks.

The last time I was in the New York Jockey Club kitchen, it was lunchtime, and Sous-Chef Richard Mikolitch was behind the first counter, with the *saucier* beside him (doubling as *poissonier*) and the meat cook beside *him*.

The next section down holds the huge stockpots and some space for the catering crew (on this particular Tuesday afternoon, one *garnisheur* making eighty club sandwiches).

Here, too, is the pastry refrigerator, holding the current day's dessert selections.

The pastry kitchen itself is upstairs on the second floor. Here the pastry cook and his assistant work, isolated from the rest of the kitchen.

In D.C., the pastry chef comes in quite early, before the kitchen gets dinnertime hot, to make the pastries for the dessert cart. His assistant comes in for the dinner shift. The assistant makes the standard menu items, and prepares the made-to-order Soufflés (recipes start on page 202).

In New York, at the time of this writing, the only dessert items are those on the menu—no pastry cart—but the menu keeps the pastry cook and his assistant busy for the full day's work.

Two flights down from the pastry kitchen (one down from the main kitchen) is the basement level. Here the butcher works, and here the pasta is made, fresh, by the pasta man. And here is the chef's office. The office is small, but no one enters without knocking.

One day, while Chef Daniel Dunas and I were in his office going over some recipes, the *poissonier* knocked, then entered with a large skinned fish in his hands. He and Chef then had a short but brisk discussion about whether it had been frozen when loaded or became frozen in the truck.

Another day, I was present when Sous-Chef Richard had a discussion over some fresh-killed duck: its quality (excellent), its freshness (still warm from the butchering), its price ($24 on the dinner menu), and what parts of the waste could be used to make a duck stock (the bones and the head).

The pace in the New York kitchen is still hectic but perhaps a bit less frenzied. There are fewer tables in the dining rooms than in D.C., but with no fewer hands, so perhaps there is a little more time. No, more time does not mean a better-prepared dish, but it may mean a dish served with more flourish.

At first glance, a busy kitchen at dinnertime might seem to be a disorganized jungle, with waiters rushing in and out, and cooks slamming back and forth. But all of this in and out and back and forth is simply the mark of a very special order in a unique world.

▪ GLOSSARY ▪

Here are some definitions of words, phrases, processes, *as I under-stand them, and as I use them in this book* (and as I heard them used by the chefs of the Jockey Clubs). This is not intended as a definitive compendium of concepts culinary (ahem). It is intended to help out the cook who may not understand some of the terms used in these recipes.

Almond flour: almonds ground very fine to the consistency of flour. This is a commercial product, and if you have any difficulty finding it, just make your own by throwing blanched almonds into your blender and processing until finely ground. They don't come out as fine, but they are good enough.

Almond paste: a combination of almond flour and sweeteners. This is the basis of Marzipan (recipe on page 208). I buy mine from a good baker in my area. Only quality shops that make their own mar-zipan are likely to carry it.

Américaine: Lobster Sauce (recipe on page 165).

Apricot glaze: See "glaze."

Aromatics: anything that smells good—herbs and spices.

Baba-au-rhum **cups:** small metal molds, about 4″ tall by about 2½″ across the top. I use them to freeze Frozen Raspberry Soufflé (recipe on page 174).

Bain-marie: a do-it-yourself double boiler; the French usually use a basin-shaped mixing bowl over a smaller pot that holds the water, or a pot in a sinkful of hot water. Excellent for heating things that then have to be beaten, like a *sabayon* (see "*sabayon*").

Baker's parchment: a specially treated paper that helps prevent sticking. Instead of being put on greased pans, Langues de Chat (recipe on page 223) are squeezed from a pastry bag onto baker's parchment (the parchment is on a cookie sheet). Not only is there no greasing, there is also no washing. Anything that makes less work for mother is welcome. The parchment can also be used for sifting: Sift onto a large sheet, then lift the edges of the sheet, and tilt into a bowl—again, much neater. A triangular piece of parchment can be cut and rolled into a "cornet" (see "cornet"). You may also see it for sale as "kitchen parchment."

Beurre manié: equal parts of butter and flour, forced together cold. Used as a thickener.

Beurre pommade: *"Beurre"* is butter and *"pommade"* is hair grease. Put them together, and you get butter that has been allowed to soften at room temperature and is the consistency of petroleum jelly. This is whipped into a dish a bit at a time, after cooking, to give it a smooth "finish." It's used in some sauces and in some soups. Once the butter goes in, the dish cannot be boiled again. Also called "flake butter."

Blanch: to boil briefly, usually for 1 to 3 minutes. Tomatoes are blanched to allow the skin to zip off; bacon is blanched to get out some of the salt; almonds are blanched to, literally, "whiten" them (and get the skins off). In blanching, the object blanched is not really cooked, just its outside.

Bloom: See "gelatin."

Bombe: an igloo-shaped dessert.

Bouillon strainer: a very fine strainer.

Bouquet garni: a combination of herbs tied together with a bit of string or tied into a bit of cheesecloth as a bag. Usually a bay leaf and a sprig each of fresh thyme and parsley.

Braise: A dish that is braised is usually cooked first at high temperature and then covered and allowed to simmer at a lower temperature.

Break: to separate. Egg whites that are beaten too much will break.

Butter and flour a pan: In baking, cake pans are often called on to be buttered and floured. A thin layer of butter is rubbed onto the inside of the pan (or melted butter is brushed on with a pastry brush), then flour is spooned into the pan. Once the flour is in, the pan is tilted, rotated, and continuously tapped, so that every bit of butter is coated with the flour. The pan is then turned over and tapped several times again, so that the excess flour falls out. There should be just the thinnest layer of flour possible to coat the butter.

Buttercream: a combination of butter, heavy cream, sugar, and other ingredients. Usually used as an icing or a filling for cake. In American baking, this is the most common icing. For a chocolate icing, I much prefer a *Ganache* (recipe on page 192).

Butterfly: a way to cut a thick filet of meat into two thinner slices. The cut is made horizontally, and the slabs of meat are "unfolded." To maintain the butterfly shape (two large wings), the meat may be left attached at the very edge.

Cake cardboard: This is a round piece of corrugated cardboard made to sit under a round cake so that it can be held during icing, lifted, etc. They come in various sizes, but I had to go to a restaurant supply store to find them.

Candy thermometer: a thermometer calibrated to tell the various stages in the making of candy (soft-ball, hard-ball, soft-crack, hard-crack). A candy thermometer is intended to stand upright in the cooking pot. Mine has a clip (with a wooden ball, so as not to burn) to keep it upright. The N.Y. Jockey Club pastry kitchen has its candy thermometer hanging by wire from the stove hood. The D.C. pastry chef does not use a candy thermometer.

Caramelize: Caramel is cooked sugar. To caramelize something, we usually dust it with sugar, and then put it under a flame briefly. The flame cooks the sugar, turning it brown and melting it.

Cèpe: an edible variety of *boletus* mushrooms, usually grown in France.

Chicken *glace:* Chicken Stock (recipe on page 155) that has been boiled until reduced (see "reduce") by half or more.

Chinois: also known as a China cap. A fine strainer, cone-shaped, with the point down.

Clarified butter: the oil part of butter, with the solids removed. Clarified butter is made by simmering butter for about a half-hour, and then pouring off the clear part—which is the clarified butter. The solids are discarded.

Coarsely chopped: to chop into pieces of no particular size or shape; as opposed to diced or finely chopped.

Cocotte: either a covered crockery pot, or a woman of ill repute. Take your choice.

Commercial product: This is a phrase I use to describe an ingredient that the Jockey Club kitchens (and other hotel and restaurant kitchens as well) purchase, already made up, from a restaurant supply house. Sauce Melba (see "Sauce Melba") is a good example of this: It can be made from scratch at home, but the restaurant kitchen buys it already made as a time-saver.

Confectioners sugar: sugar that has been ground powder-fine, and then mixed with a small amount of cornstarch (about 3%).

Coral: See "lobster coral."

Cornet: literally, a little horn. A cornet is used as a miniature pastry bag when very small amounts of stuff are to be handled—as, for example, when you want to draw a picture on the outer surface of a bombe (see "bombe") with a small amount of buttercream, in very fine lines. You can make a cornet by cutting a piece of baker's parchment (see "baker's parchment") into an isosceles triangle, 6" at the base by 12" long. Roll it into a cone with the small end closed, then fold the wide end inside the open end to keep it in shape. Fill the cone halfway with your buttercream (or whatever); cut a tiny bit of the tip off the end of the cone to open it; then fold the top over and squeeze, as you would a pastry bag.

Côte de veau: veal cutlet.

Couli: a style of cooking vegetables. Similar to a purée (see "purée") but not quite as fine and smooth. Purées are generally put through a food processor or blender; *coulis* are not.

Crimping wheel: sort of like a pizza wheel made by a drunk. It is usually used to close off the edge of pies. It cuts a wavy line through pasta.

Dash (and splash): A dash is usually a single shake, whether dry or liquid. Pepper is often given as a dash (though not in *this* book), but a liquid whose bottle has a tiny pouring spout, such as Tabasco sauce, can also be given as a dash. "Splash" usually describes a bottle being tilted, then immediately righted as fluid comes out. To me, a splash is more than a dash.

Deglaze: When meat dishes are cooked in a pan (either on the stove or in the oven), it is usually possible to make a gravy of what is left in the pan, even after the fat is poured off. To deglaze, we pour off the fat (just lift the pan and tilt and pour and discard), then return the pan to the stove. Over a medium flame, we then add a liquid— usually alcoholic, but sometimes stock, or even water. We stir this liquid into the meat juices left in the pan, scraping in the browned bits sticking to the sides or bottom, mixing it together well. This is the basis for many a gravy.

Demiglace: a thick sauce (basically a veal sauce), used to flavor other sauces (recipe on page 162).

Double cream: cream that has been reduced by half (see "reduce").

Dredge: to drag through. The British make the fish part of their famous fish-and-chips by dipping the fish filet in egg and then loading it up with flour by dragging the wet filet through the flour. The French usually just dust their filets (see "dust").

Dust: to sprinkle with a very light powdering. In those fish recipes that call for a dusting of flour, you are instructed to tap the filet to get rid of extra flour.

Escalope: a cut of meat that, to the active imagination, might look like a giant scallop.

Fines herbes: a combination of herbs, often thrown into a recipe at the very last instant before removal from the heat; usually a combination of tarragon, thyme, and parsley.

Finish: Usually, this has the connotation of a surface polish rather than a conclusion (though both senses are used in the kitchen). Butter at room temperature is beaten into a sauce to give it a finish. And, if you look at the sauce, the butter has, indeed, added a kind of satiny polish to it.

Flambé: literally, blazed. A high-alcohol-content liquor, such as cognac or a liqueur, is added to a dish and then ignited. The alcohol is allowed to burn off, leaving the flavor of the spirit behind. Maître d' Martin of Washington, D.C., told me that the flame should be "rounded," not a great pillar of fire. That great *whoosh* is not only in bad taste, but dangerous as well. He suggested that the dish be removed from the heat before the liquor is poured in, and then that the liquor be permitted to bubble in the hot dish for a few seconds before it is lit.

Fold: a gentle way to mix together two ingredients. In Concord Cake (recipe on page 184), for example, cocoa powder is folded into beaten egg whites. Some of the cocoa is sprinkled onto the surface of the beaten whites, then a spatula lifts some of the egg whites and turns them over the cocoa. This is repeated, gently, until all the cocoa is evenly distributed through the beaten whites. Ordinary mixing would really knock down the egg whites; folding does not.

Fondant: a frequent ingredient in candy recipes, made of a combination of sweeteners. Fondant is a commercial product that comes out of its tub like a thick but wet paste.

Frangelica: an almond liqueur. Quite sweet.

Fromboise: a raspberry brandy, colorless and powerful.

Fumet: a "light" stock (one that has not been cooked long enough to get full-flavored), usually fish.

Ganache: an icing made of chopped chocolate, with boiling cream poured over to melt it, then stirred gently so as not to introduce air bubbles. Really handy stuff. It makes up in minutes and will pour over any cake you may have—even if you didn't make it from one of the Jockey Club recipes (I won't tell). It solidifies, but doesn't harden like melted chocolate; it stays soft, but not sticky like chocolate sauce; and it is much faster and easier to make than buttercream. Any excess can be stored in the refrigerator and reheated for later use.

Garnish: a decorative addition to a finished dish, usually adding a flavor accent as well.

Gâteau: French for cake.

Gelatin, bloom and swell: In the Jockey Club kitchen, gelatin is allowed to sit in liquid for 10 minutes before being warmed to dissolve; this is called being allowed to "bloom" (the feeling is that it's more effective this way). When heating the liquid to dissolve gelatin, don't get it any hotter than needed to barely dissolve the gelatin powder. Most recipes call for the gelatin to go in at room temperature, and the hotter you get it, the longer you'll have to wait for it to cool. Also, boiling will solidify the gelatin, and it has to go in as a fluid.

Glace: This refers to the reduction of a fluid (see "reduce") until it is quite thick and seems almost oily.

Glaze: to give a shine to. A glaze is usually achieved by putting something meltable on a dessert (breads are sometimes glazed also): egg yolk, powdered sugar, apricot glaze, to name a few. A loaf of bread glazed with yolk and baked will shine. A *gâteau* with some apricot glaze on its surface will shine. Apricot glaze is a commercial product.

Glazed onions: See the recipe for Glazed Shallots (page 51). The same thing can be done with pearl onions.

Grand Marnier: an orange-flavored liqueur. A favorite in the pastry kitchens of both Jockey Clubs.

Grand-mère: literally, grandmother, in French. Foods prepared *grand-mère* are prepared "old-style," or "old-fashioned."

Gratin dish: a low-sided open cooking dish, usually ovenproof, in which dishes that are topped with cheese are made.

Hard-peak: See "soft-peak."

Heavy cream: whipping cream. Most of the recipes that call for cream, call for heavy cream. There are a couple of instances when light cream is used to thin something, but then it is specified.

Japonnaise: a mixture of meringue, sweetener, and flours (including nut flour) that is piped (see "pipe") from a pastry bag or spread with a spatula into whatever shape is desired, and then baked. It serves as the "cake" in a number of desserts and has a delightful texture as well as an interesting flavor.

Julienne: a style of cutting. Things prepared julienne are usually cut into long and narrow bits. Julienne potatoes can be quite long; a fine julienne can be the size and shape of paper matchsticks. Watch out for your fingers.

Juniper berries: tiny fruits of the juniper tree. They are the flavoring agent in gin. They can be picked off your own juniper tree, or you can buy them from a herb specialist.

Lamb *fond:* reduced Lamb Jus (recipe on page 164).

Leek: This close cousin to the onion looks like a scallion with a superiority complex. In cooking with leeks, we generally use only the white and the pale parts of the lower greens. Usually, the darker greens are discarded (though they can be snuck into a stock).

Lobster coral: the roe of the female lobster. This waxy, beady material turns red when the lobster is cooked: hence the "coral" name.

Marinade: a liquid, composed of herbs, spices, wine, and vinegar, in which meat (sometimes fish) is soaked (marinated) to give it flavor. The action of the marinade is almost to "cook" the meat— without any heat.

Marzipan: a combination of finely ground almonds (almond paste) and sweeteners. Marzipan is sometimes shaped into candies, but its main use in *The Jockey Club Cookbook* is as a cake covering (recipe on page 208). Sometimes called "marchpane"—but not by me.

Mayonnaise: a combination of oil, egg, vinegar, mustard, and seasonings that has been whipped enough to bring the oil to a semisolid state (recipe on page 161).

Meringue: a combination of egg whites and sugar, beaten into a thick mixture.

Mirepoix: a combination, in equal parts, of carrots, celery, and onion, chopped small. "1 cup *mirepoix*" would call for ⅓ cup of each.

Nappé : literally, covered. Chefs often refer to a sauce as cooked until *nappé* — until it coats a wooden spoon. Or a cooked piece of meat may be *nappé* with sauce.

Noisette: "*Noisette*" is a hazelnut; but "*noisette*" refers to things cut up into small pieces (about half the size of the last joint of your pinky); a "*noisette*" is a small round filet of meat; and "*beurre noisette*" is butter that has been cooked until it is a dark brown!

Parchment: See "baker's parchment."

Pastry bag: a bag, usually cloth though sometimes plastic, with a hard nozzle at one end and a wide opening at the other. Icing or batter is spooned into the wide end; the wide end is then twisted closed, which forces the batter through the nozzle. The pastry bag is used to decorate cakes or shape cookies or pipe out (see "pipe") fillings. See also "cornet."

Peppercorns: the dried round seed pods of black (or white) pepper. Peppercorns are ground, usually—either fine-ground commercially or coarse-ground in a home pepper mill. Some recipes, however, call for crushed peppercorns, and these are arrived at as follows: Place the peppercorns on a piece of parchment paper or a towel, and press and rub with the bottom of a heavy pot until the peppercorns are crushed.

Pinch: A pinch is the amount a large male chef (usually a fellow with sizable meathooks) can hold between thumb and forefinger without dusting the floor. Less than an ⅛ teaspoon, but a measurable amount.

Pipe: to use a pastry bag. Anything you squeeze from a pastry bag is referred to as "piping." In Black Forest Kirsch Torte (recipe on page 216), the rings of whipped cream squeezed from the pastry bag are referred to as "pipe rings."

Plating: putting food on the dish to serve. Plating usually describes how the elements are put together on the plate. As an example, "To plate: first the spinach purée in a collar around the dish, then some sauce in the center, then the fish on top . . . ."

Praline paste: a commercial product of ground nuts and sweetener.

Purée: a method of preparation. Foods that are puréed are cooked and then ground fine in a processor or blender. While purées are quite soft, it is important that they don't have the appearance of baby food—they should not leak when you put them on the plate.

Ramekin: a small pottery dish, usually ovenproof.

Raspberry reduction: overripe or damaged raspberries (or even good wholesome raspberries if that is the only kind you can find) cooked over a low flame until they become a thick glop. It takes 6 cups of raspberries to make 1 cup of reduction. This has great raspberry flavor, but is not sweet.

Reduce: to simmer over a low flame or to cook over a medium flame to concentrate a sauce or to thicken cream. The liquid is indeed reduced to less volume, and the flavor is concentrated as well.

Reserve: put aside for use later in the same recipe. In Watercress Soup (page 42), for example, we "reserve" a few leaves to use as a garnish, holding them apart from the cooking.

Roe: fish eggs. Caviar is roe. Shad Roes (recipe on page 95) come enclosed in a membrane. The membrane is removed after cooking.

Rough cut: to chop very coarsely (see "coarsely chopped"); to cut into big pieces.

Roux: a mixture of flour and butter, stirred together vigorously as the butter melts.

Sabayon: a recipe made with egg yolks, beaten in the top of a *bain-marie* until it thickens. The important thing with a *sabayon* is that the flame does not get too high—or you get scrambled eggs.

Sachet bag: herbs tied into a bit of cheesecloth.

Salamander: In mythology, a salamander was a lizard capable of

Salamander: In mythology, a salamander was a lizard capable of causing fires; in the Jockey Club kitchens, a salamander is a small broiling oven, used to quickly melt the top surface of a food, to brown or glaze it. Rice Pudding (recipe on page 188) is served with the top browned (the egg mix on top scorches very slightly); Fruit Torte au Grand Marnier (recipe on page 206) is glazed (the apricot glaze brushed over its surface melts very quickly). A salamander does its work in seconds. Putting things under the broiler in your oven will work about the same.

Sauce Demiglace: See "demiglace."

Sauce Melba: Named for the opera singer Nellie Melba, it is a commercial product made of raspberries and sweeteners.

Sauté: *Sauter* is, literally, "to jump." To fry something in hot butter or oil (until it "jumps") at a high or medium-high temperature.

Scant cup: about 1 tablespoon less than a level cup.

Sear: to cook at very high temperature on top of the stove. Meats are often seared before going into the oven—it's intended to keep the juices in. For example, Leg of Lamb (recipe on page 66) is placed into a roasting pan with a little oil and butter, and seared on top of the stove on all four sides before being roasted in the same pan.

Season to taste: Add salt and pepper (and sometimes lemon juice) to adjust the flavor to your own desires. This literally puts the ball in *your* court. How salty (or unsalty) do you like things? How much pepper do you want? Chef Daniel and Chef Marcel have different philosophies about seasoning. Chef Daniel expects it to come out right, and he suggests seasoning at the beginning (with perhaps another taste near the end); Chef Marcel says *of course* you must taste for seasoning at the end. You pays your penny and you takes your pick.

Serving dish: I had always thought of a serving dish as a community dish that you served *from*. However, as you can imagine, nothing in the Jockey Clubs is brought to the table "family style," and so a serving dish is that dish on which the food is brought to the table and served *on*. (Life is so confusing sometimes.)

Simmer: to cook at low heat.

Simple syrup: a combination of sugar and water in the proportion of 2:3. Most recipes call for the water to be boiled, but Pastry Chef Danny Michel of the Washington Jockey Club says that though the boiling is necessary in a commercial kitchen where the syrup is likely to sit around for a while, the sugar can be dissolved in hot tap water for immediate home use.

Slow, slowly: to cook at low temperature.

After it has boiled down, a bit of hot syrup, dripped from a spoon into ice water, can be shaped by the fingers into a small ball that readily changes shape as you press it, but doesn't fall apart. Candy thermometers (see "candy thermometer") have a listing for soft-ball.

Soft-peak: a stage in the whipping of meringue or whipped cream. As you lift your beaters out of the beaten egg whites or cream, the bit that adheres to the beater falls back to the bowl, but folds over, leaving a low rounded mound—that is soft-peak. On the other hand, if the bit that separates from the beater is upright and well defined, you have reached hard-peak. Most often, you will find yourself much more successful using whipped cream or meringue if you work it no further than soft-peak.

Sous-chef: literally, "under-boss." The sous-chef runs the kitchen under the executive chef, or without him when the big cheese is on vacation or off shift. The phrase "sous-chef" itself gives you no indication of the degree of talent or ability or training of the person. An individual who was chef in a small kitchen may take his next job as sous-chef in a big kitchen—and consider it a promotion! Most executive chefs have spent a stint as sous-chef. Most often, in the Jockey Club kitchens, it will be a sous-chef who fills in, in an emergency.

Splash (and dash): See "dash (and splash)."

Stock: a soup and sauce base usually made from the bones of lamb, beef, veal; or the head and bones of fish; or from tough fowls in the case of chicken stock. A stock is not as highly seasoned as a soup. (See, also, "*fumet.*")

Sweat: to cook briefly, until moisture appears on the outside of whatever is being cooked. In Chef Dunas' recipe for Fish Stock (page 156), the ingredients are sweated briefly before the water and wine are added.

Sweetbreads: usually the pancreas of a calf, though sometimes the thymus. In the old days, testicles were also used.

Sweet butter: unsalted butter. All of the recipes in this book that call for butter call for sweet or unsalted butter. The recipes are not standardized for salt butter.

Swell: See "gelatin."

Temper: It can be a serious mistake to add a hot ingredient to an ingredient that can curdle (such as adding hot cream to egg yolks); by first adding a few tablespoons of the hot ingredient to the cool, we warm the cool ingredient and prepare it for the heat to come. This is called tempering.

Tomato purée: tomatoes that have been peeled, seeded, and chopped, and then cooked in a small amount of oil until they break down. Tomato purée has more solids in it than does tomato paste.

Toque: the high brimless hat worn by chefs in a kitchen.

Torte: a kind of cake, usually low and cake-shaped. Where cakes usually have a little filling on a lot of cake, tortes seem to have a little cake and a lot of filling.

Tournedos: small round filet steak.

Truffles: This has two meanings. Truffles are edible fungi quite sharp in flavor, quite expensive, and quite frequently used as a garnish or to add a bit of snap to a dish. But truffles are also chocolate delicacies, made of layers of different kinds of chocolate. You should be able to tell which I mean.

Turn out: to remove a cake from a pan by turning the pan over and making gravity work for you. Sometimes a cake cardboard (see "cake cardboard") is placed over the cake before it is inverted, sometimes a towel, sometimes, if the cake is cool, just your hand. If you don't want the cake to come tumbling onto the floor or table, you'd best use something.

Vanilla bean or pod: A vanilla bean is actually the seed pod of a tropical orchid—that is one reason for its cost. Soaking it brings out the flavor. Whenever a recipe calls for a vanilla bean, heat it slowly: The longer you take heating it, the more flavor will come out. Many cooks will split the bean open, to expose more surface to the hot fluid and express more flavor. The tiny black flecks that come out are orchid seeds. No, they won't sprout in your rice pudding.

Velouté: "velvety," in French. *Velouté* is a mixture of butter, flour, and soup stock, heated and beaten until thick. It is used to thicken, for example, the pasta sauces (recipes begin on page 143). In the "nouvelle cuisine," *velouté* is a dirty word, because it is, at base, flour and butter, which practitioners of the nouvelle cuisine avoid.

Zest: the yellow (and only the yellow) of a lemon's skin.

▪ PART TWO ▪

▪ ACCOMPANIMENTS ▪

Salads

Hors d'Oeuvres

Soups

Vegetables

• SALADS •

◼▬▬▬WARM ESCARGOT SALAD (N.Y.)▬▬▬◼

The recipe as given here is for 1, but it can be easily multiplied

A warm topping to a cold mixed salad is a popular combination at the New York Jockey Club. Here we have a delightfully fragrant mixture of snails, butter, garlic, and so forth, on a bed of greens (and reds) and herbs.

You can prepare the base salad a short while in advance, but do not combine the warm and the cold elements until you are ready to serve.

Radicchio is a red-leafed salad "green," with more body than lettuce, available at specialty greengrocers. I had no difficulty finding raspberry vinegar at a gourmet shop, even out here, far away from a big city.

BASE:
bibb lettuce leaves
radicchio leaves
endive (sliced at an
    angle)

cold cooked green beans

DRESSING:
fresh tarragon, chopped
fresh parsley, chopped
fresh chives, chopped
fresh chervil, chopped

fresh basil
raspberry vinegar
olive oil
salt and pepper

TOPPING:
1 tablespoon sweet butter
8 fresh snails (out of
    shells)
½ shallot, chopped

pinch chopped fresh
    garlic
2 tablespoons raspberry
    vinegar

Tear the lettuce into large coarse pieces and lay the pieces on a luncheon plate; overlap them with similarly torn hunks of the red radicchio. Toss on a handful of cold cooked young green beans, and finish with a few slices of endive.

Combine the dressing ingredients, using about 4 times as much oil as vinegar and adjusting the herbs to your own taste.

Make the Topping: Melt a tablespoon of butter in a frying pan. Add the snails, the chopped shallot, the chopped garlic, and the raspberry vinegar. Sauté until the snails are a golden brown.

When you are ready to serve, sprinkle the dressing on the greens, and spread the warm topping over the center.

■ ■■■■■■COLD CRABMEAT SALAD (D.C.)■■■■■ ■

Serves 4

This cold salad from the D.C. kitchen is easy and quick to put together for a last-minute lunch—but very tasty.

1 pound lump crabmeat
½ cup Mayonnaise
   (see page 161)
½ cup diced celery
½ teaspoon salt
dash Tabasco sauce

bibb lettuce (for the
   plate)

¼ teaspoon white
   pepper
1¼ teaspoons grated
   onion
¼ teaspoon lemon
   juice

Drain the crabmeat and pat it dry on a clean towel. Pick over to remove any bits of shell.

In a bowl, fold together crabmeat and Mayonnaise.

Add the diced celery, salt, a dash of Tabasco, the white pepper, and grated onion, and mix together thoroughly.

Mix in the lemon juice, and taste for possible adjustment of the seasonings.

Serve on a bed of bibb lettuce.

With this salad you would likely enjoy a California Chardonnay from the Napa Valley, such as the 1982 Acacia Carneros.

Serves 4

This is very much like a chef's salad, but with a more interesting dressing.

½ head iceberg lettuce
½ small head green
  cabbage
½ small head red
  cabbage

8 ounces cooked ham
8 ounces cooked tongue
8 ounces cooked chicken
  breast
2 tomatoes

LORENZO DRESSING:
4 ounces olive oil
2 ounces wine vinegar
1 egg yolk
2 tablespoons chili
  sauce

1 teaspoon paprika
1 bunch watercress
salt and pepper

Remove (and discard) the core from the lettuce and the cabbages.

Slice the lettuce and cabbages very thin, mix together well, then divide the mixed shreds among 4 salad plates.

Julienne the meats separately, cutting them into strips a bit thicker than a matchstick. Divide each meat into 4 portions, placing 2 ounces of each, side by side, in a circle (like a sunburst) on top of the lettuce and cabbages on each plate. But leave room for the tomato slices still to come.

Core the tomatoes. Cut them in half. Then slice them in semicircles and place a semicircle or two between the different meats.

Make the Lorenzo Dressing: Whisk together the oil, the vinegar, and the egg yolk.

Whip in the chili sauce and paprika.

Clean, dry, and chop the watercress and mix in. Taste for salt and pepper.

Serve the Lorenzo Dressing in a cruet.

■■■■■■SEAFOOD SALAD (D.C.)■■■■■■ ■

Serves 4

The "crab cocktail claws" are a canned crab product, sold under that name. They are the smaller movable claws from the crab. The shell provides a tiny "handle" for the little bit of crabmeat attached. They're used here mostly for decoration—not much meat but a lot of style.

Laughlan Phillips (of the Phillips Gallery) frequently orders this work of art when he comes into the Jockey Club.

2 heads Boston lettuce	2 medium tomatoes,
8 ounces jumbo all-lump	cored, halved, sliced
crabmeat	2 eggs, hard-boiled and
2 two-pound lobsters,	quartered
cooked	1 avocado, peeled and
12 crab cocktail claws	sliced lengthwise
12 large shrimp, cooked	4 radish roses
and cleaned	12 Niçoise olives

Put whole leaves of Boston lettuce onto 4 plates.

Drain the lump crabmeat and pat it dry, then put 2 ounces on the center of each plate—on the lettuce.

Cut the lobster tails lengthwise, then into thin slices. Arrange the slices around one side of the crab and place a lobster claw beside these slices on each plate.

Arrange 3 of the crab cocktail claws and 3 of the shrimp down the other side.

Decorate each plate with semicircular slices of ½ a tomato, 2 hard-boiled egg quarters, the slices from a ¼ of a ripe avocado, a radish rose, and a few tiny, ripe, black Niçoise olives. (In the outdoor market in Avignon, you can find stalls that sell more than a dozen different kinds of olives—and you can probably find these tiny Niçoise in a gourmet shop.)

Chef Marcel and Beverage Director Bill Kennedy agree on a new-style California Chardonnay, such as Willow Hill Chardonnay, 1981. The new-style Chardonnays are more acid (which is desirable) but still fruity.

■■■■■CHICKEN JULIENNE (D.C.)■■■■■

Serves 4

The grated turnip gives this salad a delightful "snap." By the way, though the salad is called Chicken Julienne, the chicken is cubed; it is the celery root that is cut julienne. (Don't ask me—I just calls them like I sees them.)

If you have a seasonal difficulty finding celery root (also known as celeriac), I have substituted young raw kohlrabi quite successfully.

This is a favorite dish of Mrs. Art Buchwald when she visits the Jockey Club.

1 large head Boston
  lettuce
24 ounces chicken breast,
  cooked, skinned, cubed
2 cups julienne celery
  root
1 medium turnip, grated
2 medium carrots, grated
¾ cup Mayonnaise
  (see page 161)

salt and pepper
lemon juice
4 ounces cold cooked
  green beans, halved
2 eggs, hard-boiled,
  quartered
2 tomatoes, halved,
  sliced
12 Niçoise olives

Clean and drain the lettuce and divide among 4 salad plates, just covering.

In a bowl, combine the chicken, celery root, turnip, and carrots with Mayonnaise.

Mix the salt and pepper in well, and add lemon juice to taste.

Mix in the green beans.

Divide into 4 portions and serve on the lettuce. Decorate with the eggs, tomatoes, and olives.

▪ HORS D'OEUVRES ▪

At the New York Jockey Club, the menu brings you a selection of hors d'oeuvres, including some of the following—though exactly what you get will vary from season to season.

For those of you who are seeking Ratatouille, one of the tastiest of the hors d'oeuvres offered in the Jockey Club selection, do not despair; the recipe is to be found on page 48, in the Vegetables chapter.

Because there are dishes that the Jockey Clubs offer as either main course or appetizer, I have scattered them through the book, within the appropriate chapters. For example, Terrine de Canard is in the Fowl chapter on page 130; Pâté de Faisan is in Game, on page 138; Scallops and Turbot Mousse is in Shellfish, on page 111; and Quenelles of Pike and Quenelles of Salmon are in Fish, on pages 90 and 105, but I have eaten them all as the first course of the meal.

If you enjoy these hors d'oeuvres, you are in high-powered company; I am told that David Mahoney, one of New York's top executives, usually orders them when he visits the Jockey Club.

▪ ━━━━━AVOCADO SLICES (N.Y.)━━━━━ ▪

Most people tend to select avocados that are too hard and unripe. Ripe avocados are sweet, and make a delicious contrast to the piquant sauce; hard avocados are just . . . hard.

1 ripe avocado	salt and pepper
1 lemon	parsley stalks and
¼ cup olive oil	chopped parsley
¼ cup vinegar	(for garnish)

Peel a ripe avocado, slice it in half lengthwise, and remove the pit. Slice it thinly in the same direction, laying the long slices in an overlapping pattern around a serving dish.

Cut the lemon in half and squeeze the juice over the slices (this prevents blackening).

Combine the oil, vinegar, salt and pepper, and dash over the slices.

Garnish with parsley stalks in the bare center of your dish, and finely chopped parsley over the slices.

■ ■■■■■■ASPARAGUS VINAIGRETTE (N.Y.)■■■■■ ■

1 pound of fresh young asparagus
salted water

VINAIGRETTE:
1 cup olive oil
¼ cup wine vinegar

Peel the skin from the raw asparagus with a vegetable peeler, starting right below the head.

Boil for 8 minutes in salted water.

Meanwhile, whisk together the oil and vinegar until smooth.

Chill the asparagus and serve cold with the vinaigrette.

■ ■■■■■■■HARICOTS VERTS (N.Y.)■■■■■■ ■
Green Beans

I have given the recipe for 6 cups of House Dressing, because you will have many uses for this basic. Of course, the extra 5 cups should be refrigerated

Do pick over the string beans at your greengrocer to get young and tender ones. This recipe will disappoint you if mature beans with well-developed seeds are used.

1 pound young, thin string beans, trimmed
HOUSE DRESSING:
1 egg yolk
1 scant cup Dijon mustard
juice of ½ lemon
chopped parsley (for garnish)

salted water, for cooking

1 cup red wine vinegar
4 cups olive oil
salt and pepper

Boil the beans for a few minutes in salted water, and cool.

Make the House Dressing: Beat the yolk. Add the mustard and mix in.

Beat in the remaining ingredients until creamy.

Add the juice of ½ a lemon to 1 cup of House Dressing. Toss the beans and dressing together. Serve chilled, garnished with chopped parsley.

■━━━━CELERY ROOT JULIENNE (N.Y.)━━━■ ■

Celery root (also known as celeriac) is an underrated vegetable. It is at its best raw, when the crisp texture is undiminished. If you have to keep the peeled and sliced celery root refrigerated for later use, cover it with cold water to which a little lemon juice has been added.

½ pound celery root	3 tablespoons
salt and pepper	Mayonnaise
juice of ½ lemon	(see page 161)
2 tablespoons Dijon	chopped parsley (for
mustard	garnish)

Peel the celery root and slice it into thin, narrow strips.

When you are ready to serve it, drain, place on its serving platter, squeeze the lemon juice over it, and toss.

Mix together the mustard and Mayonnaise. Add to the celery root and lemon juice, and toss again.

Serve garnished with chopped parsley.

■————————COLD SHRIMP (N.Y.)————————■

As an appetizer, serve 4-6 shrimp per helping

Cook the shrimp in a pot of boiling water with a little salt and vinegar for a few minutes.

1 pound large shrimp,
  cooked, peeled,
  deveined, and cooled
1 stalk celery, finely
  chopped
salt and pepper
juice of ½ lemon

2 tablespoons ketchup
1 cup Mayonnaise
  (see page 161)
1 teaspoon Dijon mustard
chopped parsley (for
  garnish)

Toss the cooked and cleaned shrimp with the celery, salt and pepper, and lemon juice.

Mix together the ketchup, Mayonnaise, and mustard, then toss with the shrimp.

Garnish with chopped parsley.

■————————POACHED SEA BASS (N.Y.)————————■

This recipe is often made at the Jockey Club with striped bass instead of sea bass. My local seafood expert tells me that striped bass have to be 18″ to be taken, while one can find sea bass in almost any smaller size. I guess it depends on the size of the party for which you are cooking—and the size of your poacher.

1 large sea bass
  (or striped bass)
1 stalk celery
2 carrots
2 tomatoes
1 onion
bay leaf

parsley
salt
3 cups wine vinegar or
  white wine
Court-Bouillon to cover
  (see page 117)

HERB SAUCE:
½ bunch watercress
fresh tarragon
pinch chervil
2 cups Mayonnaise
  (see page 161)

juice of ½ lemon
salt and pepper

Poach the Bass: Put the bass into a poacher along with the celery, carrots, tomatoes, onion, bay leaf, parsley, salt, and wine vinegar, and cover with the Court-Bouillon. Bring to a boil, allow to cook for about 30 minutes, then let sit until the liquid is cool.

Remove from the water and allow to drain.

Remove the skin, and clean out any brown spots.

Make the Herb Sauce: Rinse a ½ bunch of watercress, and about half that amount of fresh tarragon. Do not drain.

Put into a blender with a pinch of chervil, and blend until well ground. Strain by squeezing the small amount of fluid through cloth and into the Mayonnaise (discard the green pulp).

Add the lemon juice and salt and pepper, and mix well.

Serve the bass with Herb Sauce over each individual helping.

■ ■■■■■■■CUCUMBER SALAD (N.Y.) ■■■■■■ ■

These seedless hothouse cucumbers are quite a bit larger than domestic varieties, which means that the 4 of them produce quite a few slices. If you can't get the hothouse cukes, double the number, and scrape out the seeds with a teaspoon.

The salting indicated in the recipe is to get much of the fluid out of the cucumbers. Allow the cukes to stand in the salt for a full hour, and then drain well (otherwise the recipe may come out too salty—it did turn out too salty for me the first time I tried it, because I hurried the draining time). Don't be afraid to pat the slices dry on a clean dishtowel.

4 seedless hothouse cukes	**1 cup wine vinegar**
2 tablespoons salt	**1 tablespoon Dijon mustard**
several stalks tarragon, chopped	**pepper**
½ cup olive oil	**salt (if needed)**

Peel, cut in half, and slice the cucumbers.

Sprinkle the 2 tablespoons of salt over the slices, stirring to get them all salted.

Allow to stand for an hour, and then drain off the water. (Taste here to make certain you've gotten rid of the extra salt.)

Combine with the tarragon, oil, vinegar, and mustard, mixing well and tossing all together.

Taste for final seasoning.

▪ SOUPS ▪

VICHYSSOISE (N.Y.)

Serves 4

Every French restaurant serves this traditional cold soup, but most don't serve it this creamy or this delicious. Be careful *not* to brown the leeks—that will darken the soup and make it bitter. I say that from bitter experience.

This recipe calls for fresh chives. (And for me, the only way to have fresh chives is to grow them. I keep a pot or two on a sunny windowsill in my kitchen all year round.)

2 large leeks (whites and tender greens only)	**salt and pepper**
½ stalk celery	**2 medium potatoes, peeled and diced**
1 tablespoon sweet butter	**½ cup heavy cream**
3 cups Chicken Stock (see page 155)	**fresh chives, chopped**

Chop into small pieces the whites and the tender green parts of 2 leeks (discard the tough dark-green parts) and ½ a stalk of celery, and simmer in the butter. Stir over a medium flame until the leeks are just golden—a few minutes.

Add the Chicken Stock, and salt and pepper to taste.

Add the potatoes to the stock, and cook until tender—30-35 minutes.

Allow to cool for a few minutes, then pour into a food processor or blender and liquefy.

Leave the mixture to cool. (It can be poured into a pan set in ice to cool more rapidly.)

Before serving, stir in a ½ cup cream, and then garnish each serving with a sprinkling of chopped chives.

Chef Daniel Dunas uses heavy cream, but says that light cream will serve, or even milk, if you don't want the calories.

■ ■■■■CREAM OF MUSHROOM SOUP (N.Y.) ■■■■ ■

Serves 4

This is a hot soup for the mushroom lover. The cream enhances and complements the mushroom flavor. The mushrooms used are domestic.

½ **pound mushrooms,**
 washed and drained
½ **medium onion**
1 **tablespoon sweet**
 butter
1 **tablespoon flour**
3 **cups Chicken Stock**
 (see page 155)

salt and pepper
1 **cup heavy cream**
4 **extra mushrooms,**
 sliced (for garnish)
additional butter

Chop up a ½ pound of cleaned mushrooms and ½ an onion, then simmer in butter, over a medium flame, until golden.

Sprinkle a tablespoon of flour over them, then stir in 3 cups of Chicken Stock.

Cook, uncovered, for a ½ hour, over a very low flame.

Allow to cool for a few minutes, then liquefy in a food processor or blender.

Pour back into the pan and reheat gently. Add salt and pepper to taste.

In another pan, reduce 1 cup of cream by half. Add the cream to the soup and stir.

Meanwhile, sauté the extra mushroom slices in butter until golden. Garnish each helping with a few slices.

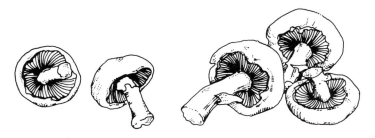

CREAM OF CELERY SOUP (N.Y.)

Serves 4

Prepare like Cream of Mushroom Soup (above), but substitute 1 cup of chopped celery for the mushrooms, and add 1 tablespoon of Béchamel Sauce (recipe on page 159) into the blender.

CREAM OF CHICKEN SOUP (N.Y.)

Serves 4

Prepare like Cream of Mushroom Soup (above), but substitute ¼ cup of diced raw chicken breast for the mushrooms, and add 1 tablespoon of Béchamel Sauce (recipe on page 159) into the blender.

CREAM OF CARROT SOUP (N.Y.)
Potage Cresci

Serves 4

This is an unusual and delicious soup.

2 carrots	**3 cups Chicken Stock**
1 medium onion	**(see page 155)**
1 tablespoon sweet	**1 medium potato, peeled**
butter	**½ cup heavy cream**
1 teaspoon sugar	**salt and pepper**

Rough cut the carrots and onion, and sauté them in butter for a few minutes.

Add the sugar and the stock, and cook, slowly, for about 20 minutes.

Dice the potato and add it, and cook for another 10-15 minutes, until the potato is tender. Allow to cool for a few minutes.

Meanwhile, boil the cream to reduce it by half.

Put the soup mixture through the blender until liquefied, then add the cream, and reheat.

Taste for salt and pepper.

SPLIT PEA SOUP
SAINT GERMAIN (N.Y.)

Serves 4

By definition, this variety of the classic French recipe *must* have a ham bone. Chef Dunas calls for the shank bone from a smoked ham or prosciutto (but he will accept smoked pork-neck bones—which are what I could find in my local markets).

Because of the soaking, this is a recipe you must start the day before. But here is a soup for which you do not need soup stock.

½ pound dried split green peas	**a smoked ham bone**
1 medium carrot	**salt and pepper**
1 medium onion, peeled	**1 tablespoon sweet butter**
3 cloves	**fried bread croutons**
1 quart water	**(for garnish)**

Soak the peas overnight in cold water.

The next day, drain off and discard the water, and rinse until clear. Put the peas into a 2-quart saucepan with the carrot and onion (stud the onion with 3 cloves). Add about 1 quart of water, the smoked ham bone, and a pinch of salt and pepper.

Cook, covered, for about an hour over a low flame. Skim off any scum on the surface.

Allow to cool for a few minutes. Remove the bone and the onion and pour the soup into a food processor or blender and liquefy. (Be absolutely certain you remove the ham bone before you put the soup into the blender.)

Reheat, and add 1 tablespoon of butter to the pot just before serving. Season to taste.

Garnish with croutons made of cubes of bread fried on all sides in butter.

■ ━━━━━━ WATERCRESS SOUP (N.Y.) ━━━━━ ■

Serves 4

Watercress is quite sharp raw, but Watercress Soup loses the sharpness while keeping the zest.

1 bunch of watercress	**3 medium potatoes,**
1 tablespoon sweet	**peeled and diced**
butter	**salt and pepper**
3 cups Chicken Stock	**½ cup heavy cream**
(see page 155)	

Wash and drain the watercress. Reserve several leaves (without stems) for later use as garnish.

Briefly sauté the watercress, stems and all, uncut, in the butter.

To the same pan, add the stock, the potatoes, about ½ teaspoon of salt, and some pepper, and cook until the potatoes are tender (about 10 minutes).

In a separate pan, reduce a ½ cup of cream by half.

When the potatoes are tender, pour the soup into a food processor or blender and liquefy. Add the cream and reheat. Taste for possible further seasoning with salt and pepper.

Garnish with the reserved raw watercress leaves.

■ ━━━━━ LEEK AND POTATO SOUP (N.Y.) ━━━━ ■
Potage Parmentier

Serves 4

Here is a delightfully hearty soup, with the potatoes cut into chunks the size of sugar cubes.

4 large leeks (whites	**3 medium potatoes,**
and tender green parts	**peeled and diced**
only)	**salt and pepper**
1 tablespoon sweet	**cream or butter**
butter	**(optional)**
3 cups Chicken Stock	**fried bread croutons**
(see page 155)	**(for garnish)**

Dice the leeks quite small, and sauté in the butter until golden.

Add the stock, the diced potatoes, and about a ¼ teaspoon of salt and some pepper to the sauté pan and cook about 25 minutes.

As an option, add a teaspoon of cream or a dollop of sweet butter before serving.

Garnish with croutons made of diced bread fried in butter on all sides.

CREAM CURRY (D.C.)
Crème Senegalese

Yields about 6 cups—enough for 5 large servings

Dishes from tropical parts of the world are often too spicy for our temperate palates. Here is a cold soup from hot western Africa (by way of the Washington Jockey Club) that is spiced just right.

4 cups Chicken Stock (see page 155)	white meat of half a chicken breast, cooked and shredded (for garnish)
1 teaspoon curry powder	
4 egg yolks	
2 cups heavy cream	parsley, chopped (for garnish)
salt and pepper	

Bring the stock to a boil, then reduce the heat to a simmer.

Add the curry and stir in.

Beat the egg yolks in a bowl for a minute; temper the yolks by stirring in about a ¼ cup of the hot stock.

Blend the cream into the yolks.

A bit at a time, add this mixture to the stock, stirring constantly. Continue to stir until somewhat thickened. *Do not allow the mixture to come to a boil—this will curdle the eggs.* (If this happens, the taste will still be fine, but the soup will look curdled.)

Taste, and add salt and pepper if needed (it will depend on the flavor of the stock).

Garnish each portion with about a teaspoon of shredded white meat of chicken and a sprinkling of chopped parsley.

CREAM OF ASPARAGUS SOUP (D.C.)

Serves 6

Don't hurry the cooking here; let it go until the asparagus are just about falling apart.

½ pound fresh
asparagus
2 tablespoons sweet
butter
1 small onion, peeled
1 leek (white and tender
green parts only)

1 medium potato, peeled
6 cups Chicken Stock
(see page 155)
1 cup heavy cream
salt and pepper
¼ cup *beurre pommade*

Wash the asparagus, and remove the pale bottom from each stalk—about a couple of inches. Remove the tips with a bit of stem, and reserve. Peel the remaining stems.

Melt the butter in a large pan, and add the onion, the leek, and the potato, all chopped coarsely.

Sauté until the onion and leek pieces are transparent. Then reduce the heat and cook for an additional 10 minutes, stirring all the while.

To the same pan, add the stock (this should be rich, flavorful stock) and the asparagus stems, and cook all together for 40-45 minutes, until the vegetables begin to fall apart.

When cooked, allow to cool for several minutes, then grind in a blender or food processor until smooth. Return to the stove and bring again to the boil.

Add 1 cup heavy cream, salt and pepper to taste, and the reserved asparagus tips, and cook very slowly for 10 more minutes.

Finish by stirring in, bit by bit, about ¼ cup of *beurre pommade* (butter at room temperature, the consistency of Vaseline), and serve. The soup must not boil again once the butter goes in.

CREAM OF MOREL
MUSHROOMS (D.C.)
Crème de Morilles

Serves 6

Morels are strange-looking but delicious mushrooms, with deeply etched ragged ridges on the outside—and a deliciously delicate flavor on the inside.

15 fresh morels	**1 quart Chicken Stock**
2 tablespoons sweet	**(see page 155)**
butter (to sauté)	**1 cup heavy cream**
4 more tablespoons sweet	**2 egg yolks**
butter (for *velouté*)	**salt and pepper**
2 ounces flour	

Chop the morels finely, and, in a 2-quart pan, sauté them in butter until just golden.

Make a chicken *velouté* by melting 4 tablespoons of butter in a separate 2-quart pot, then stirring in the flour, then mixing in the stock, over medium heat.

Add this chicken *velouté* to the morels and simmer for 30 minutes, stirring frequently.

Add the cream, and allow to return to the boil, then cook for another minute.

Stir the yolks to break them up, then add them slowly, stirring continuously. When the yolks are in, remove from the heat and taste for possible salt and pepper. The seasoning will depend on the flavor of your stock.

LOBSTER BISQUE (D.C.)

Serves about 10

I had trouble getting just plain raw lobster shells, but a local seafood restaurant/store combination was willing to sell me "lobster bodies": raw lobsters with the tails and claws removed. I substituted 5 pounds of these bodies for the 5 pounds of shells, and they worked perfectly.

5 pounds lobster shells
½ cup olive oil
½ cup corn oil
3 medium carrots
4 medium onions
1 bunch celery
2 cloves garlic, mashed
2 cups brandy
1 teaspoon cayenne
  pepper
2 cups tomato paste

1 gallon Fish Stock
  (see page 156)
8 teaspoons tarragon
1 teaspoon thyme
5 bay leaves
diced cooked lobster
  meat (for garnish)
whipped cream
  (optional)
Armagnac (optional)

In a large pot, sauté the raw lobster shells in the oils until good and red.

Chop the vegetables into chunks the size of sugar cubes, and add them. Add the garlic. Mix everything in well, and cook together, covered, for a good 10 minutes.

For safety's sake, turn off the heat. Pour in the brandy, and allow to stand for a few seconds. Then turn the stove on again (at low temperature), light the brandy, and permit the flame to burn itself out.

Add the cayenne, tomato paste, Fish Stock, fresh tarragon, fresh thyme (or dry, if you can't get fresh), and bay leaves, and reduce over a low flame by about half.

When done, strain out the solids.

Add about a tablespoon of cooked lobster meat cut into small chunks to each serving.

You may also want to add a teaspoon of Armagnac per cup of Bisque, and/or to float a teaspoon of whipped cream atop each serving.

■ ■■■■■■■SCOTCH BROTH (D.C.)■■■■■■■ ■

Serves about 10

In the cooking of the barley, a "pinch" of salt is called for. This is a good time, then, to remind you that a "pinch" is not the smallest possible bit. Yes, it is less than ⅛ teaspoon, but it is considerably more than the few grains that usually get called a pinch. A pinch is what will fit between the thumb and forefinger of an adult male chef without spilling all over the floor.

This is not a difficult soup to make, but you will have 3 different pots going at once before it all comes together. So read the recipe through before you start.

STOCK:

2-3 pounds raw lamb
    bones
water
3-4 stalks celery,
    coarsely chopped

2 medium onions,
    coarsely chopped
2 cloves

SECOND POT:

2 tablespoons butter
1 cup diced onions
1 cup diced carrots

1 cup diced celery
sachet bag of thyme leaf,
    bay leaf, 3 cloves

2 cups water
pinch salt
1 cup barley

salt and pepper
diced cooked lamb (for
    garnish)

On a roasting pan, brown the lamb bones in a 375° oven for ½ an hour or so.

Put the bones into a stockpot and cover well with water. Add the first celery, onions, and cloves, and simmer slowly for 2 hours or more—until you begin to get good flavor from the lamb.

Meanwhile, in another pot, simmer the second onions, carrots, celery, and the sachet bag in butter, at low heat, for 10-15 minutes, until the diced vegetables are just about transparent.

Add the lamb broth and cook for another ½ hour to 45 minutes.

Skim to remove the butter.

While the broth is cooking, prepare the barley by cooking it in 2 cups of water with a pinch of salt until tender. Rinse the barley to remove any extra starch.

Add the barley to the soup and cook for 5-10 minutes more. Taste for salt and pepper.

Serve garnished with a tablespoon of diced cooked lamb in each bowl.

■ VEGETABLES ■

■━━━━━RATATOUILLE (N.Y.)━━━━━■

Serves 6

In all Jockey Club recipes that include cooked tomatoes, the tomatoes are peeled and seeded first. To do this, toss the tomatoes into boiling water for a minute or so, after which they will peel easily and without waste; then core and cut them in half horizontally, and squeeze out the juice and seeds. (If the Ratatouille becomes too dry during cooking, the tomato juice, without the seeds, can be stirred in to moisten it.)

1 medium eggplant	¼ cup olive oil
2 medium zucchini	2 cloves garlic, crushed
1 green (or red) pepper	1 bay leaf
1 large onion	½ lemon
3 medium tomatoes, skinned and seeded	salt and pepper

Peel strips off the long measure of the eggplant with a vegetable peeler, and discard them. Cut all the vegetables into chunks, except the peeled and seeded tomatoes, which are chopped.

Meanwhile, in a large baking dish (preferably cast iron and enamel), heat the olive oil over a medium flame until it smokes. Then, sauté all the vegetables and seasonings in the hot oil for a few minutes.

When the eggplant is golden brown, cover the dish, and cook in a medium oven (350°-375°) for 45 minutes to an hour.

Traditionally, this is served hot, but Chef Daniel reminds us that it is delicious cold, served in a dish on a bed of crushed ice. I first tasted this Ratatouille cold, as one of the items on a platter of hors d'oeuvres, at the New York Jockey Club, and it was delicious. In fact, when I made it at home, both Floss and I preferred the taste after it had been jarred and refrigerated overnight.

SPINACH PURÉE (N.Y.)

Yields 4 small servings

1 pound fresh spinach   **dash nutmeg**
½ cup heavy cream
1 tablespoon sweet
** butter**

Pick over a pound of fresh spinach, removing the stems and any bad leaves.

Wash well and drain, but do not dry.

Put the spinach into a pan with only the water clinging to its leaves, and cook for about 3 minutes, over a medium flame, stirring occasionally to ensure even cooking.

In a saucepan, reduce the cream for about 10 minutes.

Remove the spinach into a colander and press with a spoon to get rid of excess water.

In a food processor or blender, chop fine, and return to pan.

Add the cream, butter, and nutmeg, stirring over low heat.

Cook until there is no free liquid. The spinach must not look like baby food; that is, it must not "bleed" fluid when you serve it on the plate.

ZUCCHINI WITH CHEESE (N.Y.)
Courgettes au Gratin

Serves 4

I was quite grateful to get this recipe from Chef Daniel. I always have a bumper crop of zucchini in my summer vegetable garden.

6 medium zucchini   **Sauce Béchamel (see**
1 tablespoon sweet   **   page 159)**
** butter**   **grated Parmesan cheese**

Peel the zucchini and cut them into thick slices—about ¾".

Cook in boiling salted water for 2 minutes. Don't overcook: They must stay firm.

Drain them.

Melt the butter in a frying pan, and fry the slices on both sides, until they are a golden brown.

Put them flat into a gratin dish (a low-sided ovenproof dish).

Coat the surfaces with Sauce Béchamel, and sprinkle with grated cheese.

Cook for 5 or 6 minutes in a medium oven (350°-375°).

■■■■■■■■■■■CÉLERI AU JUS (N.Y.)■■■■■■■■■■

Serves 2

4 stalks of celery	3 ounces white wine
sliced pork back fat	3 ounces rich Chicken or
½ an onion, sliced	Beef Stock (see page
½ a carrot, sliced	155)
2 garlic cloves	2 tablespoons tomato
1 bay leaf	sauce
salt and pepper	

Cut 4 celery stalks into 5″ pieces. Wash, and remove any bad leaves.

Scrape away the outer surface with a vegetable peeler (to get rid of the strings).

Boil the celery in salted water for about 10 minutes, then remove and drain.

Into a pan put a few slices of pork back fat, then the sliced onion and carrot, the garlic, and a bay leaf.

Place the celery on top, and salt and pepper.

Cook on top of the stove for a few minutes over a medium flame.

When the vegetables start to color, add the wine and stock.

Cover the pan, and cook until tender, about 20-25 minutes. When tender, remove from the fire.

Pour the liquid into a saucepan; skim and discard the fat.

Stir 2 tablespoons of tomato sauce into the skimmed liquid, and reheat.

Place the celery on a dish, and pour this sauce over it.

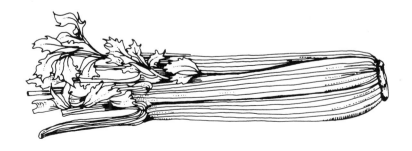

■━━━━━GLAZED SHALLOTS (N.Y.)━━━━■ ■

About 5 servings

Any stock you have on hand (or in the refrigerator) would be appropriate for cooking this vegetable.

2 or 3 dozen shallots, peeled	**½ teaspoon sugar**
1 tablespoon sweet butter	**½ cup stock or water**
	salt and pepper

Peel the shallots and put them into a frying pan with the butter.

Sprinkle in the sugar, and cook briefly to allow the shallots to caramelize (the sugar turns dark brown).

Add the stock, or water, and put the pan, uncovered, into a 300° oven to cook until all the liquid is completely reduced and the shallots have a nice brown color (about 30 minutes). Taste for salt and pepper.

■ ━━━━━POTATOES DAUPHINE (N.Y.)━━━■ ■

Serves 6

Once cooked, the potatoes in this recipe can either be forced through a ricer, pressed through a heavy strainer with the back of a strong spoon, or put through a *chinois* (a metal strainer shaped, supposedly, like an inverted Chinese hat).

3 or 4 medium potatoes, peeled	**4 large eggs**
4 tablespoons sweet butter	**few dashes nutmeg**
½ cup water or milk	**salt and pepper**
⅜ cup flour	**1 tablespoon grated Parmesan cheese**
	½ cup olive oil

Halve or quarter the potatoes and cook in salted water until tender (about 25 minutes).

Drain them and force through a sieve.

Into a pan, put the butter and water (or milk), and bring to a boil, then remove from the fire.

Mix in the flour, and cook over a low flame, stirring constantly for 2 or 3 minutes.

Remove from the fire.

One at a time, add the eggs, stirring well.

Mix in the potatoes, the seasonings, and grated cheese, and taste.

In a large frying pan, heat the oil. The oil must be hot when you put in the first bits of mixture, but not so hot that it scorches.

Using a spoon, drop 1 walnut-sized chunk of the potato mixture at a time into the hot oil.

As it browns, turn the ball onto its uncooked side.

The puffs should double in size as they cook.

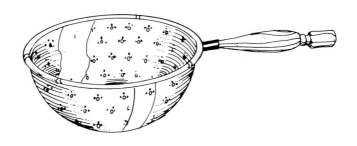

■ ■■■■■■POTATOES LYONNAISE (N.Y.)■■■■ ■

Serves 4

5 or 6 medium potatoes, cooked (skins on)	**4 ounces onions, peeled and finely sliced**
4 tablespoons sweet butter	**chopped parsley (for garnish)**

Peel and slice the cooked potatoes.

Melt the butter in a pan, and put in the sliced onions.

Cook very slowly, stirring frequently. When they are a nice golden color, remove the onions and drain them on a plate, leaving the butter in the pan.

Put the potato slices into the butter, and cook them over a low fire until a golden brown. Then add the onions, and continue to cook together for a few more minutes.

Sprinkle with chopped parsley just before serving.

RICE PILAF (D.C.)

Serves 4

For this recipe, I use a 2-quart cast-iron and enamel pot (with a cover for when it goes into the oven).

Chef Marcel feels that most home cooks are too shy about salt when it comes to rice. He says that the amount of salt for your rice should be the same as you use for potatoes.

½ shallot, chopped
1 tablespoon sweet
  butter
2 cups Chicken Stock
  (see page 155)
1 cup uncooked white
  rice

1 bay leaf
salt
chopped tomato and
  chives (for garnish)

Preheat your oven to 375°.

Simmer the finely chopped shallot in butter until transparent (do not brown).

Add the Chicken Stock and the rice and stir. (This is regular, not instant, rice.)

Add the bay leaf, and up to 2 teaspoons of salt if needed (that will depend on your stock).

Cover and slowly bring to a boil on the top of the stove.

When it comes to a boil, remove from the stove and set in a preheated 375° oven, and cook for 18 minutes. After 18 minutes, remove, still covered, and allow to stand for another 10 minutes.

When 10 minutes is up, remove the lid and loosen the rice with a fork.

Serve garnished with chopped tomato and chives.

CHESTNUT PURÉE (D.C.)

Serves 4-6

1½ pounds chestnuts
  (in shells)
milk (to cover)
1 cup chopped celery
1 tablespoon sweet
  butter

salt and pepper
sugar (if needed)
plain whipped cream
  (if needed)
dash nutmeg

Preheat your oven to 350°

Put the chestnuts into a pot of water on top of the stove, and cook for 10-15 minutes. Drain, allow to cool briefly, and peel off the shells and skins.

Put the peeled chestnuts into a pan and barely cover with milk. Simmer for 20 minutes, or until the chestnuts are quite soft.

Drain in a colander.

Discard the milk and grind the chestnuts in a food processor or blender until quite smooth.

Remove and set aside.

Now put the chopped celery into the processor and chop it even smaller (or mince it by hand).

Sauté the celery in butter until quite tender, then add the ground-up chestnuts, salt and pepper to taste, and a pinch of sugar if needed. Also, if you find the purée somewhat dry and thick (that will depend on how fresh the chestnuts are), stir in 1 or 2 tablespoons of unsweetened whipped cream.

Finish by stirring in a dash of nutmeg, then bake in a 350° oven for about 10 minutes.

BRAISED CELERY (D.C.)

Serves 4

The deep cuts into the base of the celery bunch help this thicker part to cook at the same rate as the rest. (The cuts also indicate the later division into 4 portions.)

1 bunch of celery
Chicken Stock (see
  page 155)

½ cup Demiglace
  (see page 162)
grated Swiss cheese

Trim off the darkest outer stalks of the celery, then cut away the tops, about 7"-9" from the base. Finally, cut a cross about a ½" deep into the base of the bunch.

Cook just covered with Chicken Stock, over a medium-low flame, for about a ½ hour.

When cooked, drain and cool, then cut lengthwise into quarters. (The stalks of each portion are still connected when the celery is served.)

Put into a dry pan, then add some Demiglace and cook over a low flame for about 10 more minutes.

Grate a little Swiss cheese over the surface and brown briefly under a salamander or broiler just before serving.

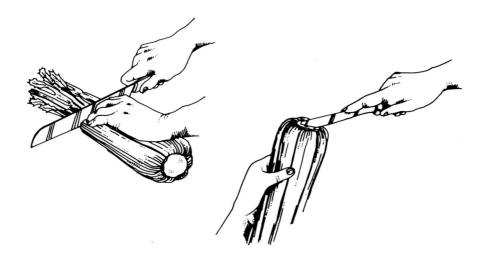

POMMES SOUFFLÉS (D.C.)
Puffed Potatoes

Yields . . . as many as you feel like frying

These are slices of potatoes that puff up, a bit like slightly elongated footballs. I understand that Julio Iglesias sings their praises—at least he usually orders them with his Jockey Club dinner.

Soups: Vichyssoise, Cream of Mushroom, and friends

Assorted Hors d'Oeuvres: Poached Sea Bass, Asparagus Vinaigrette,
Cold Shrimp, Ratatouille, Celery Root Julienne

The potatoes are cut into thin ovals, about ⅛" thick, but about 3½" long and 1½" wide.

In the mid-nineteenth century, Baron James de Rothschild threw a Parisian bash for a few hundred of his most intimate friends, to celebrate the opening of his new railroad. Well, the story goes that the train was late, and so his chef (the world-famous Chef Carene, former chef to Czar Alexander and England's prince regent) took the half-fried potatoes out of the oil, held them aside, then finished the frying as the train pulled in. And, guess what? Pommes Soufflés were invented!

In the Jockey Club kitchen, they use two deep-fat fryers, with the temperatures at the two different settings.

corn oil
potatoes

Figuring about 4 or 5 pieces per serving, peel and shape the potatoes.

Heat about 3" of corn oil in a fryer or a pot to 350°, and put the potatoes in. Shake the container.

When they start to swell a little, remove from the oil, and refrigerate until they are wanted. When the half-cooked potatoes come out of the oil, they will collapse some.

When you are ready to serve, heat the oil to 450°-500°. Drop in enough for 1 serving (4 or 5 pieces), and cook for *15 seconds,* or until just golden brown.

If you wish to cook them all at once, Sous-Chef David Biela says you have to keep shaking them while they fry.

▪ PART THREE ▪

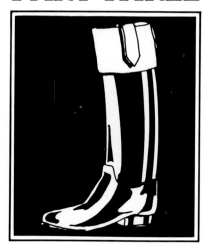

▪ MAIN COURSES ▪

Meats

Fish

Shellfish

Fowl

Game

Pasta

Sauces and Stocks

Radicchio, endive, bibb lettuce, and watercress
make an excellent base for many salad toppings

Cold Crabmeat Salad

▪ MEATS ▪

━BEEF STEAK AND━ KIDNEY PIE (N.Y.)

Serves 4

When Chef Daniel gave me this recipe, he said that the kidneys were to be cut into ¼″ slices; when I watched the dish being prepared in the kitchen a week later, the sous-chef insisted that the kidneys be cut into *chunks*. Both came out delicious; it's a matter of taste.

The arrowroot starch and sherry called for at the end of the ingredients list is to thicken the sauce, if thickening is needed. The starch is dissolved by stirring it into the sherry (or water). Jockey Club chefs prefer arrowroot to cornstarch for thickening. Arrowroot is also considered to be an aid to digestion. If you can't find arrowroot in your supermarket, try a health-food store.

This is a dish with its roots in England, and British rock-star Rod Stewart usually orders it when he visits New York and the Jockey Club.

¾ pound calf or beef kidneys	bouquet garni (see page 156)
2 pounds beef steak	1 tablespoon arrowroot starch, optional
2 tablespoons flour	¼ cup sherry (or water), optional
salt and pepper	
3 ounces sweet butter	
1 medium onion, chopped	Flaky Pastry (see page 166)
Beef Stock (see page 155)	

Clean the kidneys, removing all tubes and fat and membranes. Cut the kidneys into ¼″ slices.

Cut the beef steak into 1½" cubes.

Mix the kidneys and beef with the flour and some salt and pepper.

Melt the butter in a saucepan and sauté the onion until golden.

Add the meat, and brown, stirring constantly.

Moisten with a little Beef Stock.

Add more salt and pepper, and a bouquet garni.

Cover and simmer for 1¾ hours or until the meat is tender.

If the liquid is too thin, thicken with a tablespoon of arrowroot starch mixed with ¼ cup of sherry or water.

Transfer to an individual ovenproof dish, allow to cool, and cover with a Flaky Pastry top. (A piece of Flaky Pastry about the size of a golf ball, rolled thin, will give you your top.)

Bake only until the pastry is brown, about 20 minutes.

John Benevento recommends a "sturdy" California Cabernet Sauvignon from Beaulieu Vineyards, 1979.

■ ■CORNED-BEEF HASH (N.Y.)■ ■

The actual quantity of meat and potatoes you use will depend on the weight of the corned beef you can find. In any case, begin preparation by cooking the beef and the potatoes the day before.

1 corned beef	**pepper**
potatoes, unpeeled	**1 tablespoon sweet**
1 medium onion	**butter**
2 tablespoons heavy	
cream	

Cover the piece of corned beef with water and boil it for 3 or 4 hours, in a covered pot. Allow it to cool in the same water (to absorb the juices), then refrigerate overnight.

Boil an approximately equal volume of whole potatoes until tender (but not soft), jackets on; remove from the water, and refrigerate overnight.

Peel the potatoes. Chop the potatoes and meat into small bits in equal parts, and mix.

Chop an onion into small bits, and mix in, along with the cream. Pepper to taste.

Melt the butter in a frying pan, and when the pan is hot, spoon in helpings of the chopped hash, and flatten to a patty shape.

Fry on both sides until crisp and brown outside but creamy inside.

Serve with a poached egg on top of each helping.

Beef Steak and Kidney Pie (with a Flaky Pastry crust)

Corned-Beef Hash

■■■■■■VEAL CHOP GRAND-MÈRE (N.Y.)■■■■ ■

Serves 1

To blanch the bacon called for in this recipe, drop it into boiling water for a few minutes, then remove, allow to cool, and dice.

When Floss, my wife, was in the New York Jockey Club, she looked at the menu, read "Veal Chop Grand-Mère," and asked the waiter, "What is 'Grand-Mère'?" meaning, what style is it cooked in. The waiter explained: " 'Grand-Mère' is a grandmother." A great help. Generally speaking, dishes prepared "Grand-Mère" are said to be cooked in an old-fashioned style.

1 large veal rib chop per person
salt and pepper
2 tablespoons butter
a few mushrooms, sliced
6 small Glazed Onions (see page 19)
3 small potatoes, diced
2 ounces smoked bacon, blanched and diced

½ cup Veal Stock (see page 157)
¼ teaspoon chopped fresh tarragon
¼ teaspoon chopped fresh thyme
sprig fresh tarragon

Season the chop with salt and pepper, then sauté it in the butter until golden brown on both sides—a few minutes per side.

Add a few sliced mushrooms, the Glazed Onions, the potatoes, and the bacon.

Simmer everything for about 10 minutes over a low flame, uncovered.

To make the gravy, remove the chop from the pan, add the Veal Stock and the chopped tarragon and thyme. Stir in and reduce by about half. After a couple of minutes, add a sprig of fresh tarragon, cook for 3 more minutes, and pour over the chop.

With this dish, a robust California Cabernet Sauvignon is recommended, such as the 1981 vintage from Robert Mondavi Winery.

■■■■■■■ROAST LEG OF LAMB (N.Y.)■■■■■ ■

This recipe is for lamb in the French style—which refers not only to the herbs, but also to its rareness. Chef Daniel Dunas, in fact, says that sometimes the French like their lamb a little *too* rare. If you would like your lamb a bit better done, add 15 minutes to the cooking time.

a leg of lamb	1 tablespoon butter
(7-9 pounds)	2 tablespoons olive oil
rosemary	1 carrot, diced
thyme	1 medium onion, diced
salt and pepper	water or stock
3 cloves garlic	(for gravy)

Preheat your oven to 400°.

Trim the leg: Remove the fat, the membrane just over the meat, the skirt, and any bone ends that the butcher has half cut off. (When I last made this dish, I weighed the fat I trimmed off, and it came to 13 ounces of fat trimmed from a 9-pound leg.)

Season the leg by rubbing it with rosemary, thyme, salt and pepper, and by slitting it in 3 widely separated places and inserting a clove of garlic in each slit.

In your roasting pan put a tablespoon of butter and 2 tablespoons of olive oil, and heat on top of the stove.

Put the leg in the pan, uncovered, and sear for about a minute on each of the 4 sides.

Put into the oven, still not covered, and roast at 400° for about 1 hour. Baste frequently, and keep the leg cooking evenly by giving it a quarter turn every 15 minutes.

When you think the leg is done, you can test it. Take a big tapestry needle (or a thin metal knitting needle), and stick it into a thick part of the leg. Look at the juice that comes out. If it is bloody-red, then you probably want to cook it a bit more.

When cooked, remove the pan from the oven, put the leg onto a carving board or platter.

Begin the gravy by draining the fat from the roasting pan and braising the vegetables in the remaining lamb juices.

While cooking the vegetables, deglaze the pan by adding a little water or stock and scraping the brown bits from the sides of the pan into the vegetables.

Cook until the vegetables are done, but still crisp.

Serve the lamb with this gravy and the braised vegetables.

With this recipe, try a red Bordeaux, such as the 1979 vintage from Château Giscours in Margaux.

Veal Chop Grand-Mère

"Welcome to the Jockey Club"

FILET MIGNON IN WHITE WINE SAUCE (D.C.)
Filet Mignon au Vin Blanc

Serves 2

Timing is important with all filet dishes: They cook quickly and cool quickly. Prepare the sauce before the filets are cooked. The sauce should be ready to spoon over the meat as it comes out of the broiler.

SAUCE:

½ cup dry white wine	**2 tablespoons sweet**
1 shallot, chopped fine	**butter, at room**
1 tablespoon tomato	**temperature**
paste	**fresh-ground pepper**
½ cup beef consommé	**salt**
2 eight-ounce filets	**parsley, chopped (for garnish)**
	1 scallion, cut thin on bias (for garnish)

In a saucepan combine the wine, shallot, tomato paste (or homemade tomato purée), and consommé. Cook until reduced by at least half.

Remove from the heat, and add the butter a bit at a time, stirring. The sauce should not boil once the butter is added.

Taste; and adjust the flavor with fresh-ground black pepper and salt, if needed.

Broil the Filets: Sous-Chef Tom Kelman suggests the meat be browned on the first side, then turned and browned, then stood on edge and browned, then reversed and browned. By the time all 4 sides are browned, you have a rare filet.

Spoon the sauce over the filets, then garnish with fresh chopped parsley and the white and pale green parts of a spring onion (scallion) thin-cut on the bias.

With this filet dish, try a red Burgundy, such as Château Greysac Médoc, 1979.

■■■■■VEAL CUTLET WITH HERBS (D.C.)■■■■ ■
Côte de Veau Fines Herbes

Serves 1

Figure on 6 to 8 ounces of veal cutlet per serving.

1 veal cutlet **salt and pepper** **2 tablespoons sweet** **butter**	**3 tablespoons white** **wine**
FINES HERBES: **1 sprig tarragon** **½ teaspoon chervil** **½ a walnut-size** **shallot** **1 teaspoon parsley** **1 teaspoon chives**	**(all herbs are fresh and** **all are chopped fine)**

Season the cutlet with salt and pepper.

Melt the butter in a *cocotte* or a cast-iron and enamel frying pan.

Fry the cutlet on both sides, about 1-1½ minutes per side.

Reserve on a warm dish.

Deglaze the pan with the white wine, mixing the brown bits in well.

Add the herbs, stir, then remove from the heat.

Pour the sauce over the cutlet and serve.

A red Bordeaux would go very nicely with this dish, Château Pontet Canet-Pauillac, 1976.

Tournedos Rossini

Red Snapper Belle Meunière

Serves 1

This recipe as given below serves 1; when I serve 2, I double the amount of meat, but keep the other ingredients the same.

The filet should be pounded with a mallet until it is about ¼" thick.

This is a dish prepared at tableside, and Maître d' Martin gave me his feelings about dishes *flambé* at the table. The idea is to keep the flame "rounded," not to have an explosion. Anything more is dangerous (and "flashy"). He controls the size of the flame by removing the pan from the heat just before adding the Armagnac. After adding the brandy, he allows the sauce to boil for a moment in the hot pan. He *then* returns it to the flame, and tilts it gently, to allow the flame to ignite the alcohol fumes.

Be sure you don't prepare this dish under a smoke detector.

1 filet mignon, about 8 ounces, cut butterfly, pounded thin	**1 shallot, finely chopped**
	¼ cup Beef Stock (see page 155)
Dijon mustard	**½ teaspoon additional Dijon mustard**
salt and pepper	
2 tablespoons sweet butter	**2 splashes Worcestershire sauce**
¾ cup Armagnac	**1 tablespoon cream**
1 additional tablespoon butter	**1 teaspoon chopped fresh parsley**

Coat the steak lightly with Dijon mustard, both sides, spreading it on with the back of a fork.

Season with salt and pepper.

Melt the butter in a copper pan over medium-high heat.

Sauté the steak, on both sides: about 1 minute per side for rare; 1½ minutes for medium.

When done, add the Armagnac as described above and *flambé* until all the flame is gone, then remove the steaks from the pan. Tilt the pan to allow the liquid to run to one side, then add a tablespoon of butter to the dry side, and sauté the shallot until brown.

Pour in the Beef Stock, and stir all together.

Stir in a ½ teaspoon of mustard and the Worcestershire sauce.

Add the cream and parsley, and stir.

Put the steak back in the pan, and warm for a moment on both sides.

Serve with the sauce spooned over the steak.

Martin suggests a red Burgundy, Laboure-Roi, Gevrey-Chambertin, 1979.

■■■■■■■TOURNEDOS ROSSINI (D.C.)■■■■■■ ■

Serves 1

Here again, Chef Marcel insists on *real* Madeira wine.

1 large crouton
1 seven-ounce filet
    mignon
4 tablespoons sweet
    butter
½ cup Madeira wine
½ cup Demiglace (see
    page 162)

1 teaspoon butter, at
    room temperature
1 teaspoon chopped
    truffles
1 slice cooked goose
    liver

Make a crouton by cutting a slice of bread to the size and shape of your filet and sautéing it in butter until golden.

Fry the filet in 4 tablespoons of butter—about 1 minute per side (at medium-high flame) for rare; about 1½ minutes per side for medium.

Place the steak on the crouton on the serving plate.

Discard the butter and deglaze the pan with the Madeira, then reduce until as thick as oil.

Add the Demiglace and boil for a few minutes.

Turn off the flame and finish with a teaspoon of butter at room temperature, stirred in well.

When finished, add 1 teaspoon of finely chopped truffles, lay a slice of cooked goose liver on the filet, and coat everything with the sauce.

To double the recipe, add one more steak, one more crouton, another teaspoon of truffles, and another slice of goose liver. All else can stay the same.

A red Bordeaux would go nicely with this dish. Try a Château Palmer, Margaux, 1976.

Quenelles of Pike in Champagne Sauce

Cold Lobster Parisienne

VEAL SWEETBREADS IN LEMON BUTTER (D.C.)
Ris de Veau Maréchale

Serves 1

Figure on 6 to 7 ounces of sweetbreads for a serving.

1 pair of sweetbreads
salt and pepper
flour
1 egg
½ cup milk
fine bread crumbs
2 tablespoons sweet
    butter

2 tablespoons lemon
    juice
asparagus spears (for
    garnish)
truffles, sliced (for
    garnish)

Soak the sweetbreads in cold water overnight.

Blanch them (drop them into boiling water) for 10 minutes.

Remove, allow to cool, and clean (see page 146) under running cold water. Pat dry on a towel.

Cut into ¼" slices.

Season with salt and pepper, and dust lightly with flour. Shake off any excess flour.

Mix the egg and milk together, and dip the slices in, then into the bread crumbs for a light covering.

Heat 2 tablespoons of butter in a sauté pan until light brown (this is *beurre noisette*). Mix in the lemon juice, and sauté the slices at a medium heat. (If the flame is too high, the crumbs will cook dark brown before the slices of sweetbreads are done.)

Garnish the sweetbreads with cooked asparagus spears and a slice of truffle.

■━━━━━━━PEPPER STEAK (D.C.)━━━━━━■
Steak au Poivre

Serves 2

cracked black pepper
2 eight-ounce sirloins
2 ounces corn oil
4 ounces cognac
2 ounces Dry Sack Sherry
4 ounces Demiglace
  (see page 162)

4 ounces heavy cream
2 tablespoons sweet
  butter, at room
  temperature
salt and pepper

Crush half a dozen or so peppercorns (put them on parchment or foil, then crush with the bottom of a heavy pot), and lightly cover the steaks with the bits.

Sauté the sirloins in the oil until done (about 5 minutes per side for medium), then remove to serving plates.

Pour off the fat: Grasp the pan firmly and tilt, allowing the fat to pour slowly into something you can discard. The fat floats to the surface, and you can see the difference between the fat and the meat juices.

Deglaze with the cognac (stir the juices and any hard bits in the pan into the liquor), and add the sherry.

Reduce until the sauce coats a wooden spoon.

Add the Demiglace, then reduce again, add the cream, and reduce to *nappé*.

Whip in the butter, and taste for seasoning.

Divide in 2 and serve over the meat.

A red Bordeaux is recommended with Steak au Poivre: for example, Saint-Estèphe Cos d'Estournel, 1966.

Interior of t

C. Jockey Club

MEDALLIONS OF VEAL IN MUSHROOM SAUCE (D.C.)
Mignons de Veau aux Champignons

There is enough sauce in this recipe for 5 servings. If your group is smaller, the extra sauce can be saved and stored

The morels called for are dried mushrooms, and the chanterelles are fresh; either may be available at gourmet shops. The domestic mushrooms can be any other fresh wild mushroom. Canned chanterelles (or *cèpes*) can be used if the fresh are unavailable.

Morels are interesting-looking things, shaped like tiny closed umbrellas, with deep veining on their surface. The recipe calls for a total of 1 cup of dried morels. Remove the stems from enough to make ½ cup of whole caps. Quarter the remaining morels and add the discarded stems to make the second ½ cup.

SAUCE (for 5):

3 cups heavy cream	½ cup dried morels, quartered
1 tablespoon finely chopped shallots	½ cup good brandy
2 tablespoons sweet butter	¼ cup Madeira
½ cup fresh chanterelles	salt and white pepper
½ cup domestic mushrooms, quartered	2 tablespoons sweet butter, at room temperature
½ cup dried morels (caps only)	

2-ounce medallions of veal (2 per serving)   **2 tablespoons butter, to sauté**

Simmer the cream in a saucepan until it is reduced by half.

Meanwhile, soak the morels briefly (to remove the sand), then strain them.

Put the shallots into a sauté pan with 2 tablespoons of butter, and sauté until just transparent.

Add the fresh mushrooms (chanterelles and others) and shake the pan.

Add the morels (the whole caps and the bits) and cook halfway— about 2 minutes.

Add ¾ of the brandy, warm it briefly, and *flambé* (see page 18). When the flames die, add the Madeira.

Cover the pan and cook at medium heat until the mushrooms "sweat"—express a little moisture on their surface. Then remove the cover and reduce the liquid down to almost a glaze on the bottom of the pan.

Add the reduced cream, bring back to the boil, and allow to reduce, if necessary, until the sauce coats a wooden spoon.

Season with salt and pepper and add the rest of the brandy.

Strain the mushrooms out, put the sauce into a blender, and blend until quite smooth.

Put the sauce into a *bain-marie* or double boiler, and whip in the 2 tablespoons of butter. Then return all the mushrooms to the sauce. Hold in the *bain-marie* until the meat is ready.

Allowing 2 medallions (of 2 ounces each) for a serving, sauté the veal in butter a couple of minutes per side, until done.

Serve coated with the sauce.

With this dish you might want to serve a red Burgundy, such as Volnay Saint Enots, Premier Cru, Prieur-Brunet, 1978.

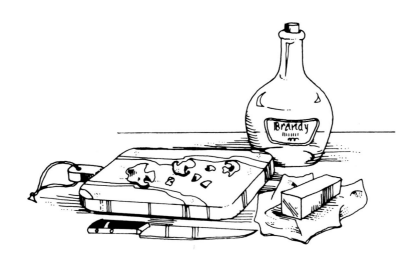

Scallops Orléannaise

Pâté de Faisan en Croûte

■■■■■■■■VEAL SALTIMBOCCA (D.C.)■■■■■■■■

The veal is for 1 person, but the sauce and duxelles are for 4 or 5 servings

I do not find veal in itself very tasty, but here is an extremely flavorful dish, combining veal, Parmesan cheese, and a mushroom sauce. The Mushroom Duxelles should be started first—it can be prepared in advance—then the sauce, then the veal. I describe the making of 1 helping of veal, but the duxelles and sauce are enough for 4 or 5 servings.

MUSHROOM DUXELLES:
1 tablespoon sweet
   butter
1 tablespoon minced
   onion
10 ounces mushrooms,
   washed, then chopped

1 tablespoon minced
   shallots
juice of ⅓ lemon
   (optional)
salt and pepper

SAUCE:
2 tablespoons corn oil
1 cup *mirepoix* (mixed
   onions, carrots, celery,
   chopped fine)
mushroom trimmings
   (from the caps, below)
2 cups Marsala
1 cup Demiglace
   (see page 162)

1 cup Chicken Stock
   (see page 155)
salt and pepper
2 cups sliced fresh
   mushroom caps,
   sautéed in
   butter (garnish)

MEAT:
6-ounce veal cutlet,
   pounded thin and large
Mushroom Duxelles
pinch fresh sage
1 teaspoon freshly grated
   Parmesan cheese

flour
salt and pepper
2 thin slices prosciutto
   ham
2 tablespoons sweet
   butter

Prepare the Mushroom Duxelles: Sauté the onions in butter until transparent, then reduce the flame to very low, add the mushrooms, and cook until dark brown and almost dry—perhaps as long as 45 minutes. After about 20 minutes, add the shallots. Finish with salt and pepper.

Optionally, you can add lemon juice with the shallots.

Make the Sauce: Brown the *mirepoix* and mushroom trimmings in oil.

Deglaze by stirring in the Marsala, and reduce until quite thick.

Add the Demiglace and Chicken Stock, stir in, and reduce until the sauce coats a wooden spoon.

Strain, and taste for salt and pepper.

Make the Veal: Take your pounded cutlet and coat the top of it with a few tablespoons of Mushroom Duxelles mixed with sage and Parmesan cheese. (Chef Marcel says that if it is a "good" Parmesan—fresh ground from imported cheese—1 teaspoon is enough; if it is one of the milder prepackaged domestic concoctions, you will need 2 teaspoons.) Place the prosciutto slices on top, to cover the duxelles. Fold the cutlet in half, and trim to make it even.

Sauté for 3-4 minutes per side at medium heat, then another 3 minutes per side at low (total: 7 minutes cooking).

Serve the veal coated with the sauce and garnished with mushrooms sautéed in smoking-hot butter until golden brown.

With this dish the Chef suggests an Italian dry red wine, such as a Barolo.

STEAK TARTARE (D.C.)
Raw Chopped Filet Mignon

Serves 1

Allow 8 ounces of ground filet mignon per person. The ingredients and instructions given are for 1 serving. At the D.C. Jockey Club, one of the captains will make this raw-meat dish at your table. Sorry, but no fireworks.

2 teaspoons Dijon mustard	2 splashes Worcestershire sauce
salt and fresh-ground black pepper	2 dashes Tabasco sauce
1 egg yolk	8 ounces filet mignon, ground
3 ounces olive oil	dash cognac
1 teaspoon whole capers	dash white wine
1 teaspoon chopped onion	additional parsley, chopped (for garnish)
1 teaspoon chopped parsley	

Into a large salad bowl, put the mustard, a little salt, some fresh-ground black pepper, and an egg yolk.

Stir well with a fork.

Slowly drip in 3 ounces of olive oil, mixing briskly with the fork to thicken it into a mayonnaise as you pour. Mix until almost firm.

Add the whole capers (don't even crush them or the combination of caper juice and onion will be bitter), the onion, parsley, and the sauces.

Mix well into the mayonnaise.

Add the meat and mix everything together with 2 forks.

When mixed, add the alcohols, and mix again. Maître d'Hôtel Martin warns against trying to mix the alcohols with the mayonnaise.

Move the mixture to the serving dish and, with the forks, mold it into a rectangular shape — like a steak.

Score the "steak" with the back of a fork, and garnish with some chopped parsley.

▪ FISH ▪

FILETS OF SOLE BONNE FEMME (N.Y.)

Serves 2

The egg yolks called for in this recipe are made *"à la sabayon"*: That is, they are put into the top of a double boiler, over barely simmering water, and whipped briskly until quite thick, creamy, and pale—*but not cooked.*

8 filets of sole
salt and pepper
1 tablespoon sweet
  butter
3 shallots, chopped fine
1 cup chopped
  mushrooms
1 cup dry white wine
Fish Stock (see
  page 156)
buttered parchment or
  brown paper (for
  cover)

additional sweet butter
  and flour (optional, for
  beurre manié)
2 tablespoons whipped
  cream
2 egg yolks (made
  à la sabayon)
chopped parsley (for
  garnish)

Preheat your oven to 375 °.

Wrap the filets in some plastic wrap and flatten them by hitting them with the flat of a cleaver or a heavy knife. Remove the plastic.

Season the filets with salt and pepper, lay them in a buttered baking dish, and sprinkle with the shallots and mushrooms.

Add the wine and some Fish Stock (to barely cover the fish).

Cover the dish with a piece of buttered paper, and bake for about 10 minutes at 375°.

Remove from the oven, take off the paper, and drain the liquid into a small pan.

Reduce the liquid by about two-thirds. If necessary, thicken the sauce with a little *beurre manié* (made by mixing together, until smooth, equal quantities of unmelted butter and flour).

Bring the sauce to a boil and add the whipped cream and the thickened egg yolks, and stir well.

Arrange the filets on a serving dish, covered with the mushrooms and garnished with some chopped parsley.

Pour the sauce over the surface and place under a salamander or broiler to brown.

For a wine, try a 1979 Alsatian Riesling by Hugel.

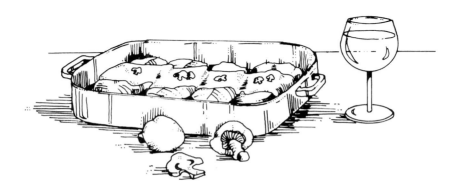

▪ ▬▬▬▬QUENELLES OF PIKE▬▬▬▬ ▪
AU CHAMPAGNE (N.Y.)

Yields about 12 quenelles

The subtle flavor and airy texture of this dish are bound to impress anyone. Pike is a fine-textured fish, and the addition of the Choux Paste makes it positively fluffy. At the New York Jockey Club, these are served as an appetizer, with 2 quenelles per helping. But the recipe easily doubles, and it can make a main course for 5 or 6.

If you have any personal questions about this dish, ask Ann Landers: I am told that this is a favorite of hers when she comes to the Jockey Club.

CHOUX PASTE:

1 cup milk
7 tablespoons sweet
  butter
1 teaspoon sugar

pinch salt
1 scant cup flour
4 eggs

SAUCE CHAMPAGNE:

½ cup champagne
2 shallots, finely
  chopped
½ cup Fish Stock
  (see page 156)

2 tablespoons
  sweet butter, melted
1 tablespoon flour
2 tablespoons heavy
  cream

QUENELLES:

½ pound pike filets
2 egg whites
salt and pepper
½ cup Choux Paste

½ cup heavy cream
Fish Stock (see page 156)
Sauce Champagne

Make the Choux Paste: Choux Paste is called for when we want something to puff up during cooking. In this case, we want the quenelles to swell as they simmer.

Pour the milk into a heavy pan, add the butter, sugar, and salt, and bring to the boil. When the mixture boils, remove it from the heat.

With a wooden spoon, stir in the flour.

Return to the fire, and cook, stirring continuously, for a minute or two, to dry it somewhat.

Still stirring, remove from the heat again, and, one at a time, stir in the eggs.

This yields about 2 cups of Choux Paste; that's more than you need for this recipe, but the excess can be stored in the refrigerator for several days.

Make the Sauce Champagne: Put the champagne and shallots into a pan with the Fish Stock, and reduce by a good quarter. It doesn't matter whether the champagne is domestic or imported.

Heat the butter and gently stir the flour into it, making a roux.

Add the champagne mixture to the roux, stir, and cook for a few more minutes.

Stir in the cream and continue cooking for a few more minutes.

Yields over 1 cup of sauce: enough for the quenelles.

(For a lighter sauce, add a few tablespoons of whipped cream at the end.)

Make the Quenelles: In a meat grinder or food processor, grind the pike until quite fine.

Place a bowl on ice and add your fish.

One at a time, mix in the egg whites, then add the salt and pepper, and the Choux Paste.

Gradually mix in the heavy cream.

Using 2 soupspoons, shape the mixture into oval-shaped quenelles.

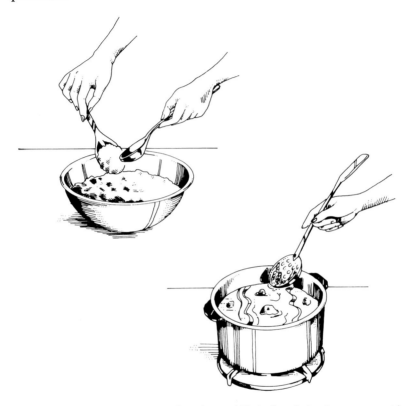

Poach them in a couple of inches of Fish Stock (or hot water, if you are desperate) in a large skillet for about 8 minutes on one side, then 2 minutes on the other. Remove with a slotted spoon, then drain them on cloth. The stock should barely simmer. Too active a boil breaks off bits of the mixture. Handle the cooked quenelles carefully: They are very delicate—in texture as well as flavor.

Put them in a pan with some hot Sauce Champagne and let simmer for another 5 minutes.

As you might guess, a champagne goes very well with these quenelles: perhaps a non-vintage Perrier-Jouet Grand Brut from Épernay.

■━━━━━━RED SNAPPER━━━━━━■
BELLE MEUNIÈRE (N.Y.)

Serves 1

Anything prepared *"meunière"* (literally: the miller's wife) is floured and cooked in butter. This is "Belle Meunière," which means that this miller's wife is beautiful—probably because she cooks in even more butter.

Red snapper is a delectable fish. Bought whole, it is filleted for you on the spot. Have your fish man fillet it close to the bones.

The recipe is given as it is prepared at the Jockey Club—cooked individually for one person. But when I make it at home for the two of us, I use a large skillet that holds 2 filets. I double the rest of the ingredients, but I don't increase the butter.

1 slice red snapper (about 8 ounces)
salt and pepper
flour
2 tablespoons sweet butter (for fish)
1 tablespoon finely chopped fresh parsley

2 tablespoons sweet butter (for mushrooms)
1 ounce mushrooms, sliced thin
1 tablespoon butter (for lemon)
juice of ½ lemon

Salt and pepper the snapper, and dust it lightly in flour (do not dredge).

Melt the butter in a large pan, and when it is hot, put in the snapper.

Sauté the fish until golden brown, about 2 minutes on each side, over a medium flame.

Put the fish on its dish and sprinkle on the parsley.

Discard the butter in the pan. Melt another 2 tablespoons of butter and sauté the mushrooms until golden. When the mushrooms are cooked, pour them with their butter over the fish.

Melt another tablespoon of butter and add the lemon juice, and pour this lemon butter over the fish.

Bring to the table and serve immediately.

For your wine, you would probably enjoy a 1983 California Johannesberg Riesling from Joseph Phelps.

■ ═══════COLD POACHED TROUT WITH ■■■■■ ■
PINK MAYONNAISE (D.C.)

Serves 6

This is extremely easy to make. When I was traveling back and forth between New York and Washington, D.C., I could make this dish and leave a few of the trout for Floss to have while I was away. In answer to your question, No, Floss has not cooked since I took over 20 years ago. If I don't cook, she tends not to eat.

6 whole brook trout
white wine

PINK MAYONNAISE:

1 cup Mayonnaise (see page 161)	**1 teaspoon grated lemon zest**
⅓ cup tomato paste	**salt and pepper**
juice of ½ lemon	

GARNISH:

cucumber slices	**sprigs of fresh tarragon**
thin lemon slices	**hard-boiled egg quarters**

Clean the trout (or have them cleaned) but leave on the heads and tails.

Put them in a pot just large enough, covered with white wine. Poach them by bringing the wine to a boil and then simmering for 10 minutes. Drain the fish when cooked and allow them to cool.

Arrange them on a cold platter and chill them in the refrigerator.

Make the Pink Mayonnaise: To 1 cup of Mayonnaise add the tomato paste and lemon juice and stir in well.

Stir in the lemon zest.

Add salt and pepper, if needed.

When the Mayonnaise is finished and the fish are chilled, remove the trout from the refrigerator.

Peel the skin from the trout, but be sure to leave on the heads and tails.

Coat each individual plate with some Pink Mayonnaise. (Serve the extra Mayonnaise in a gooseneck cruet.) Put 1 fish on each plate.

Garnish each with a slice of cucumber, a slice of lemon, a spray of tarragon, and a quarter of a hard-boiled egg.

With this simple dish, try a 1981 Muscadet Château-de-Chasselsoir from the Loire Valley.

■ ━━━━━━━━FRESH SHAD ROE ━━━━━━ ■
WITH BACON (D.C.)

Serves 1

Figure 1 set (2 roes) per serving. In this recipe, the *fines herbes* are ¼ teaspoon each of finely chopped parsley, tarragon, chervil, chives, and basil.

1 set of roes	***fines herbes***
salt and pepper	**2 slices bacon, cooked**
1 tablespoon	**crisp**
sweet butter, melted	

Season the roes with salt and pepper.

Sauté in melted butter over a medium flame, browning on both sides until done. (To test for doneness, press a finger gently into the thickest part of the roe; if done, it will feel firm.)

When cooked, remove the ligaments.

Place on a serving dish and sprinkle the finely chopped herbs over the roes. Serve with a slice of crisp-cooked bacon on each roe.

Another Loire Valley wine might go well with this recipe: a 1982 Vouvray Château Moncontour, for instance.

■ ━━━━━ TURBOT FILET WITH TOMATOES ━━━━ ■
AND WINE (D.C.)
Suprême de Turbot Duglere

Serves 2

Turbot is my favorite fish. When not overcooked, its texture and flavor are just suited to my palate.

1 stick sweet butter	**1 pound turbot filet**
1 tablespoon chopped	**salt and pepper**
parsley	**1 cup dry white wine**
2 medium tomatoes,	**chopped parsley (for**
peeled, seeded,	**garnish)**
chopped	
1 shallot, chopped	

Preheat your oven to 375°.

Dot the bottom of a tightly covered baking pan with butter, and sprinkle on the parsley, chopped tomatoes, and finely chopped shallot.

Place the turbot in the pan, over the vegetables, and season with salt and pepper.

Cover with about a cup of dry white wine.

Cover the pan and cook for 15 to 20 minutes at 375°.

Divide the fish onto 2 plates and spoon some of the sauce on each. (If the sauce is too thin, reduce it in a saucepan.)

Garnish with more chopped parsley.

With this turbot dish, try a 1981 Pouilly-Fumé, de Ladoucette.

■ ■■■■■■■SAUTÉED TROUT WITH■■■■■■ ■ PROSCIUTTO (D.C.)
Truite Sauté Ardennaise

Serves 1

A half-pound trout serves 1 person. It will take about 2 thin slices of prosciutto to make the julienne.

1 trout
2 tablespoons sweet butter
¼ cup fresh bread crumbs
¼ cup julienne (cut fine) prosciutto ham (about 2 slices)

4 teaspoons sweet butter
1 tablespoon chopped fresh parsley

Cut off the head and tail and sauté the trout in butter until it's a golden brown.

Remove from the pan and arrange on a serving plate.

In the same pan, sauté the crumbs until a light brown.

Add the prosciutto and stir, until warm.

Add 4 additional teaspoons of butter, and melt.

Add the parsley, stir in, and pour over the trout.

To multiply the recipe, just increase everything in proportion, except for the original sautéing butter. This can be increased by 1 tablespoon of butter for each additional trout.

Chef Marcel suggests for your wine a Gewürztraminer from Alsace, such as the 1981 from Trimbach.

■ ■■■■■■■■SALMON ESCALOPE (D.C.)■■■■■■■ ■

Serves 1

When you cut the salmon into 3 pieces, those chunks don't look like scallops, but they are traditionally called *escalopes*.

Beurre pommade, as a reminder, is butter at room temperature, about the texture of petroleum jelly.

8 ounces of salmon filet
salt and pepper
flour
2 tablespoons sweet butter
4 teaspoons *beurre pommade*
½ a large shallot, chopped fine

1 teaspoon chopped parsley
1 teaspoon chopped chives
1 sprig tarragon, chopped
½ teaspoon chopped chervil

GARNISH:
thin lemon slice　　　　**thin cucumber slices**

Slice the 8-ounce salmon filet at an angle into 3 pieces.

Salt and pepper and flour each very lightly. (Hold up the salmon and tap to get off excess flour.)

Sauté the fish in 2 tablespoons of butter. Start at medium-high heat and reduce the flame to low when the salmon is colored on both sides (1 minute at high per side, then 8-10 minutes on slow, altogether). Remove the salmon to a plate and discard the butter.

Into the same pan, put the *beurre pommade*. When it begins to foam, throw in the herbs, shake the pan, and pour it over the fish.

Serve garnished with a slice of lemon and a couple of thin slices of cucumber.

The suggested wine with this dish is a light Chablis Grand Cru les Clos, 1981, from Moreau.

■ ■━━━━━BAKED RED SNAPPER FILET━━━■━━━■ ■
WITH CRABMEAT (D.C.)

Serves 4

When you use crabmeat always remember to drain off the liquid and pat the crabmeat dry on a clean towel.

The recipe calls for a piece of buttered paper. This is a piece of parchment paper (almost as big as the pot) that has been rubbed with butter. The paper is placed over the fish, and the steam is held in—but not as tightly as it would be with a pot cover.

When the fish is cooked and you prepare the crab sauce, do it quickly. The snapper is cooling while you dally.

2 tablespoons sweet butter	**fresh-ground pepper**
1 shallot, chopped fine	**⅔ cup white wine (Chablis)**
pinch salt	**buttered paper**
4 skinless red snapper filets (8-10 ounces each)	**8 ounces crabmeat**
	salt and pepper
juice of 1 large lemon (divided in 2)	**2 tablespoons chopped fresh parsley**

Preheat your oven to 350°.

Butter a baking pan.

Sprinkle the pan with the shallots and a pinch of salt.

Place the skinless filets in the pan, and season with half the lemon juice and fresh-ground pepper. Add the wine to the pan.

Spread the buttered paper (buttered side down) over the fish.

Bake for about 15 minutes at 350°.

Transfer each baked fish to an individual dish and pour the liquid into a skillet. To the skillet add the crabmeat and the remaining lemon juice, and salt and pepper to taste.

Sauté the crabmeat until hot, then spoon it over the fish filets.

Sprinkle with chopped fresh parsley.

■ ▬▬▬BROOK TROUT PROVENÇALE (D.C.)▬▬▬ ■

Serves 4

4 fresh trout, boned salt and pepper flour	**4 tablespoons sweet butter**

SAUCE PROVENÇALE:

3 tablespoons olive oil
**1½ tablespoons chopped
   fresh garlic**
**1 tablespoon chopped
   shallots**
**1½ cups crushed fresh
   tomatoes, peeled and
   seeded**
½ cup white wine
	**½ cup Demiglace
	   (see page 162)**
	**¼ pound butter, at
	   room temperature**
	**2 tablespoons chopped
	   fresh parsley**
	salt and pepper

Season the inner side of each trout with salt and pepper. (The inside is where the bones were.) Dip the fish into flour, and shake and pat each piece to get rid of the excess flour.

Pan fry the trout in 4 tablespoons of butter, over a medium flame, covered, until done—about 4 minutes per side.

Make the Sauce Provençale: Heat the oil over a high flame in a saucepan, and add the garlic and shallots. *Do not brown them.*

Add the tomatoes, and shake the pan (still at high temperature).

Shake again and add the wine.

Stir in the Demiglace, then lower the flame.

Whip in the butter, and add the parsley. The sauce must not boil once the butter is in.

Season with salt and pepper.

Pour the sauce over each fish and serve.

With this dish you would probably enjoy a white Côtes-du-Rhône. Try the 1980 Vernay from Condrieu-Viognier.

■■■■■SALMON WITH LEEK SAUCE (D.C.)■■■■■
Salmon au Coulis de Poireaux

Serves 4

LEEK SAUCE:
2 bunches of leeks
¼ pound sweet butter
2 cups vermouth
2 cups heavy cream

salt and pepper
Fish Stock or Chicken
Stock, to thin (see
pages 156 and 155)

FISH:
1 thick 2-pound salmon
filet (skinned)
flour

2 tablespoons sweet
butter

Make the Leek Sauce: Chop the leeks (all the whites and about a quarter of the greens) and sauté in butter until transparent—do not brown.

Add the vermouth, and reduce until almost dry.

Add the cream and bring to a boil, and reduce by about half.

Add salt and pepper to taste.

The sauce should be thick enough to just coat a spoon. If it is too thick, add a little light Fish Stock or Chicken Stock. If too thin, reduce further.

Make the Fish: Slice the salmon horizontally, and then vertically in half (the Jockey Club kitchen always uses thick salmon filets) to give you four 8-ounce filets. Flour each lightly, then sauté them in butter over a medium-high flame, cooking the cut side first (this will be the showing side when you serve it).

When done, pat dry with a clean towel and serve on a bed of the Leek Sauce.

Beverage Director Bill Kennedy suggests a Côte de Beaune, such as the Saint-Aubin from R. Clerget, 1976. Chef Marcel agrees.

■■■■■SUPREME OF SALMON POACHED■■■■■
WITH JULIENNE VEGETABLES,
SAUCE BEURRE BLANC (D.C.)

Sauce serves 5

Assume you'll want one 8-ounce filet per person. The vegetables called for are cut into slivers about the size and shape of paper matchsticks. The shallots are chopped.

FISH:
filets of salmon   **Fish Stock (see page 156)**

SAUCE BEURRE BLANC:
½ cup sherry wine vinegar   **2 tablespoons julienne truffles**
1 cup dry white wine   **2 tablespoons finely chopped shallots**
2 cups heavy cream
½ cup julienne leeks (whites only) **1 pound *beurre pommade* (sweet butter at room temperature)**
½ cup julienne carrots
½ cup julienne snowpeas   **salt and white pepper**
½ cup julienne celery

Poach the salmon in Fish Stock, barely simmering for about 10 minutes, or until firm in the center of the filet.

Meanwhile begin the Sauce Beurre Blanc by combining the vinegar and wine and reducing over a medium flame until almost dry.

Add the cream and reduce by half.

Add the vegetables and cook until crunchy—they should still be firm—and then strain them out and put aside.

Reduce the cream further, until only about a ¼ cup remains, then lower the flame.

A bit at a time, whisk in the very soft *beurre pommade.*

Once you begin to add the *beurre pommade,* it is important that the sauce not boil again—however, it must stay warm enough to serve. (In the Jockey Club kitchen, the chefs keep the pot on the side of the stove—which is quite hot, but not hot enough to boil. For the home kitchen, use a *very* low flame.)

Season the sauce with salt and white pepper to taste, then add the vegetables again.

Spoon over the poached filet to serve.

Chef Marcel recommends a Vin d'Alsace Gewürztraminer Trimbach 1981; Bill Kennedy suggests any good California Chardonnay such as Château Bouchaine, Alexander Valley, 1981.

■ ■■■■■■POACHED RED SNAPPER WITH■■■■■ ■
CURRY SAUCE AND GINGER SAUCE (D.C.)
Red Snapper Poche aux Deux Sauces
Curry Américaine and Ginger Beurre Blanc

Serves 2

Fumet is a very light Fish Stock (the recipe is on page 156). *Mirepoix* is a mixture of chopped vegetables, in equal measure.

FISH:

2 filets of red snapper, 6 ounces each

white wine and *fumet* to cover

CURRY AMÉRICAINE:

1 cup *mirepoix* (onion, carrot, celery, chopped)
¼ pound sweet butter
2 tablespoons peeled and diced green apple
¼ thinly sliced banana
1½ tablespoons Madras

2 tablespoons fresh coriander
1 cup Chicken Stock (see page 155)
1 cup *Américaine* Sauce (see page 165)
½ cup heavy cream
salt and white pepper

BEURRE BLANC:

2 cups white wine
1 shallot, chopped
1 cup cream
2 tablespoons chopped fresh ginger

½ pound butter, at room temperature
1 tablespoon lime juice
salt and white pepper

Poach the Fish: To poach the filets, just simmer them, barely covered, in a combination of white wine and *fumet* (equal parts) until they are firm at their thickest part. Remember, barely simmer them, do not boil.

Make the Curry: To begin the curry, sweat the *mirepoix* in the butter: That is, cook briefly, over high temperature, until moisture forms on the vegetables.

Add the fruit and cook briefly.

Add the curry powder and coriander.

Deglaze with a cup of Chicken Stock (mix everything in well), and cook over medium heat until reduced by half.

Add the *Américaine* Sauce, and bring back to the boil.

Add ½ cup cream and reduce again, until the sauce is *nappé* (coats a wooden spoon).

Remove from the heat and process briefly in a blender.

Pour the blended mixture through a fine strainer. (Discard anything fibrous left in the strainer.) Season to taste.

Make the Beurre Blanc (Butter Sauce): Combine the wine and shallots in a saucepan, and reduce to almost a glaze.

Add 1 cup cream and reduce by half.

Add the ginger, and reduce about a quarter further.

Remove from the flame, add the room-temperature butter, and whip it in.

Finish with lime juice and salt and pepper to taste.

Plating: First, put some Curry *Américaine* on the plate, then the snapper, then coat the fish with the Butter Sauce. Swirl the 2 sauces where they combine on the plate.

To complement this flavorful dish, try a California, Grand Cru Vineyards, Gewürztraminer, 1983.

■■■POACHED SALMON WITH 2 PEPPERS■■■ ■ AND CHIVES BUTTER SAUCE (D.C.)
Salmon Poche aux Coulis de Deux Poivrons
Sauce Beurre de Ciboulette

Serves 4

The look of this dish is very important: The purées of red pepper and green pepper are placed on the dish in the shape of crescent moons; the salmon is placed between them.

Buttered parchment is called for to cover the fish while poaching. This is parchment paper (available in supermarkets) that has been rubbed with a thin layer of butter. It is placed over the poaching fish to hold the steam in. (In the Jockey Club kitchen, they sometimes use the wrapping paper from 1-pound bars of butter.)

For poaching, any frying pan or saucepan large enough to accommodate the fish will do.

3 large red bell
   peppers
3 large green bell
   peppers
¼ pound sweet butter
1 cup Chicken Stock
   (see page 155)
½ cup heavy cream
salt and pepper
butter, for pan
2 shallots, chopped fine
4 salmon filets,
   6 ounces each

2 cups dry white wine
buttered parchment
SAUCE BEURRE:
½ cup heavy cream
¾ pound sweet butter,
   at room temperature
1 tablespoon chopped
   fresh dill weed
salt and pepper (again)
4 tablespoons chopped
   fresh chives

Keeping the colors separate, clean and chop the peppers.

In separate pans, with 4 tablespoons of butter each, sauté the peppers over a very low flame until soft (about 10 minutes). Do not brown at all.

When soft, add half the stock to each pan, and continue to cook until almost dry.

Scrape separately into a blender and purée until smooth (about the texture of baby food), adding about ¼ cup of heavy cream to each. Be sure not to mix the colors.

Add salt and pepper to taste.

Butter a pan for poaching. Sprinkle the shallots over the bottom of the pan, add the fish, and cover about ⅔ with the wine, and place a piece of buttered parchment over all.

Cook until the filets are firm at their thickest parts—about 10 minutes at the simmer.

Sauce Beurre de Ciboulette: When the fish is done, remove the paper, and drain the liquid into a saucepan. Add a ½ cup of cream, and reduce over a medium-high flame by half.

Reduce the flame to its lowest, and whip in ¾ of a pound of butter a bit at a time. (The sauce must not boil once the butter goes in.)

When all the butter is in and the sauce is smooth, add the dill and taste for salt and pepper.

Finish by adding the chives.

Plating: Divide both color peppers into 4 parts, and decorate 4 dishes as follows: Spoon the red-pepper purée down one side of the dish, in the shape of a quarter-moon; repeat with the green down the other side. Put a little sauce between them, lay down the filet, and coat with more sauce.

You would enjoy a white Burgundy with this dish. Chef Marcel recommends a Pouilly-Fuissé, Château de Beauregard, 1982; or try a Puligny-Montrachet, Remoissenet, 1979.

■ ━━━━QUENELLES OF SALMON WITH━━━■ TRUFFLE BUTTER SAUCE (D.C.)

Makes enough for a large dinner party

This delicious appetizer is the brainchild of the 2 sous-chefs in the D.C. kitchen, Tom Kelman and David Biela. I watched Tom shape these small quenelles one evening while he was supervising dinner and answering my questions all at once. It was lovely to watch his precise movements. You can give it your whole attention.

The salmon need not start out as expensive filets; trimmings would be fine, so long as it's all fish.

All the ingredients and all the utensils must be very cold—almost freezing—before starting.

QUENELLES:
- 2 pounds salmon
- 1 tablespoon chopped shallots
- 1 ounce cognac
- 1 tablespoon salt
- 1 teaspoon white pepper
- 1 egg
- 2 egg whites
- 2 cups heavy cream
- 1 tablespoon Worcestershire sauce
- ¼ teaspoon cayenne
- 1 cup heavy cream (for whipping)
- salt and pepper
- 1 gallon Fish Stock (for poaching, see page 156)

VIN BLANC SAUCE:
- ½ cup Noilly Prat dry vermouth
- ½ cup *Fumet* (see page 156)
- 1 tablespoon finely chopped shallots
- 1 pint heavy cream
- salt and white pepper to taste

TRUFFLE BUTTER:
- ½ cup Madeira
- ¼ cup brandy
- ¼ pound truffles, chopped fine
- 2 tablespoons Chicken Glace (reduced Chicken Stock, see page 155)
- 1½ pounds sweet butter, at room temperature

Mixing the Fish: In a food processor, grind the salmon and shallots together until fine.

Add the cognac, and the salt and pepper. Mix in well, then place the processor container in the freezer for a ½ hour.

Remove, put back in place, and purée at high speed. Stop, scrape down the insides of the container with a spatula, and purée again.

Add an egg and process for a minute; scrape down the inside again; add the egg whites, and process for another minute.

Scrape down the sides, turn on the machine, and, very slowly, add 2 cups of cream.

Add the Worcestershire sauce and cayenne.

Transfer to a mixing bowl and refrigerate for an hour.

Whip 1 cup of cream to soft-peak, and fold it into the mixture.

At this stage, you have to make a sample so that you can taste for final adjustment of the seasonings.

Bring a little of the Fish Stock to a simmer, and spoon a small amount of the quenelle mixture in. Allow it to cook, without boiling, for about 15 minutes.

Taste the cooked quenelle, and if needed adjust the uncooked mixture with salt and pepper.

Refrigerate overnight, in its mixing bowl.

Shaping the Quenelles: To shape the fish mix into quenelles, you will need 2 large tablespoons, a container of boiling-hot water, and Fish Stock just barely simmering over low heat.

Take the mixing bowl holding the fish mixture out of the refrigerator. Place one of the spoons in the hot water. Fill the other spoon with fish mixture, and drag it up the side of the bowl (scraping away some of the mixture, condensing what remains in the spoon), forming an oval shape.

Remove the spoon from the hot water, and scoop the mix from the cold spoon to the hot. Heat the empty spoon, and scoop back and forth, keeping the quenelle warm and moist, until it reaches a football shape.

As shaped, drop gently into the hot Fish Stock and allow to poach for 10-15 minutes without boiling, turning them as they cook.

As the quenelles are cooked, remove from the water and reserve.

Vin Blanc Sauce: Combine the vermouth, the *Fumet*, and the chopped shallots, and reduce to a glaze.

Reduce a pint of heavy cream by half, add to the vermouth glaze, blend together, and taste for seasoning.

Truffle Butter: Combine the Madeira and brandy, and reduce by three-quarters.

Add the truffles and the Chicken Glace, and cook for 2 minutes. Allow to cool a bit.

Transfer to a mixing bowl, and beat in the 1½ pounds of butter. When completely mixed, it's done.

To make Truffle Butter Sauce, combine 2 parts of Truffle Butter to 1 part Vin Blanc Sauce.

To serve, heat the quenelles by simmering for another 10 minutes; coat the plate with about 2 tablespoons of Truffle Butter Sauce; remove the quenelles from the water and quickly pat dry with a clean towel; serve on the sauce.

The quenelle recipe should make about 40-50 quenelles. The sauce should be enough for about 2 tablespoons of sauce per helping.

With this chef-d'oeuvre you will very likely enjoy a 1981 Bâtard Montrachet, from the Clerget Vineyards.

▪ SHELLFISH ▪

AVOCADO FILLED WITH CRAB (N.Y.)

The sauce serves 4. Each avocado serves 1

Here is a cold appetizer that is easy to prepare, delicious, and handsome to serve.

ROSEMARY SAUCE:
4 ounces Mayonnaise
(see page 161)
2 tablespoons ketchup

½ ounce cognac
1 ounce whipped cream
salt and pepper

AVOCADO:
1 avocado per serving
bibb lettuce and chicory
leaves, for plate
3 tablespoons lump
crabmeat, drained,
per serving

Rosemary Sauce
chopped capers and
parsley (for garnish)

The Rosemary Sauce: Mix together all the sauce ingredients until smooth.

The Avocado: Cut off the top half of the avocado and discard it. Remove the pit. Cut a bit off the bottom so that it stands firmly. Do not peel.

Decorate the plate with leaves of bibb lettuce and chicory, stand the avocado in place, and fill with lump crabmeat.

Cover the crab with the Rosemary Sauce, and garnish with a few chopped capers and chopped parsley.

CRAB CAKES JOCKEY CLUB (D.C.)

Serves 2. These patties are quite rich, and 2 are plenty for a main course

The crabmeat must be free of extra fluid; you can drain it through a colander, and then spread it on a clean dry kitchen towel and pat it dryish. As with all crab recipes, you want to pick over the meat for shells and other hard bits.

This is a popular dish. Maître d'Martin tells me that this is the choice of many celebrities: Carol Burnett, Anthony Quinn, Warren Beatty, and Walter Cronkite all order Crab Cakes when they dine at the Jockey Club. I was in the D.C. kitchen one night, and by 8:50 the *poissonier* had filled 26 orders.

1 egg
1 egg yolk
4 teaspoons Fish Velouté
   (see page 110)
1 teaspoon Dijon mustard
½ teaspoon
   Worcestershire sauce
1 pound lump crabmeat

1 slice white bread,
   crumbed
salt and white pepper
   to taste
flour (for dipping)
3 or 4 tablespoons sweet
   butter

Beat the egg and yolk briefly.

Add the Fish Velouté, mustard, and Worcestershire sauce.

Combine the crabmeat and the bread crumbs (I make the bread crumbs in my blender—very simple) with the egg mixture.

Taste for salt and pepper.

Divide into 4 parts and shape each into a patty.

Dip each patty lightly in flour and fry in the butter for 7 minutes per side over very low heat. The outside should be golden, but not hard; the inside should be quite moist.

For a wine selection, Chef Marcel suggests a white Bordeaux, such as Château Carbonnieux, 1982 Grand-Cru Graves.

■■■■■BAKED CRAB JOCKEY CLUB (D.C.)■■■ ■

Serves about 12 as an appetizer

This dish is usually made as an appetizer, but it can be served with a simple Rice Pilaf (recipe on page 53) as a main course for 4.

FISH VELOUTÉ:
4 tablespoons butter
scant ½ cup flour

2 cups Fish Stock
(see page 156)

CRAB:
2 cups heavy cream

1 pound lump crabmeat

Preheat your oven to 350°.

Make the Fish Velouté: Over low heat, melt the butter in a saucepan; stir in the flour; heat briefly to remove starchy taste; add the Fish Stock, stirring until the mixture is fairly thick.

The Crab: Remove the *velouté* from the flame and stir in the heavy cream.
  Drain the crabmeat, and pat dry on a clean towel. Stir the crabmeat into the mixture. Bake in the saucepan at 350° for about 10 minutes. The center should bubble slightly.
  Glaze briefly under the broiler until the surface is golden brown.

■■■■■CRABMEAT SAUTÉ NORFOLK (D.C.)■■■ ■

Serves 4 as a main course

Here is a crab dish with a little more snap to it. Chef Marcel says not to crush the capers, so I use small ones.

1 pound lump crabmeat
3 tablespoons sweet
   butter
1 teaspoon finely
   chopped shallots
2 teaspoons whole capers
2 tablespoons lemon
   juice

salt and pepper
1 tablespoon chopped
   parsley
4 teaspoons
   Worcestershire sauce

Drain the crabmeat, then pat it dry on a clean towel.

Sauté the crabmeat in the butter until golden brown.

Add and stir in the shallots, capers (whole, remember), and lemon juice. Taste for the addition of salt and pepper.

Finish by stirring in the parsley and Worcestershire sauce.

With this piquant dish, your wine might be a 1982 Sancerre, Clos de la Crele, from Domaine Lucien.

■ ■■■■■SCALLOPS AND TURBOT MOUSSE■■■■ ■ WITH BASIL SAUCE (D.C.)

Yields enough for 30-40 servings

The blender in my home kitchen would not process all the fish at once; I had to do it in 3 batches.

This is a spectacular and delicious appetizer, served cold. The Basil Sauce is actually a mayonnaise.

5 pounds scallops
1½ pounds turbot
8 egg whites
2 whole eggs
5 teaspoons salt
2 teaspoons white pepper
½ teaspoon ground
   nutmeg
1 quart heavy cream

BASIL SAUCE:
6 egg yolks
salt
⅓ ounce white pepper
1½ tablespoons wine
   vinegar

6 ounces raw lobster
   meat, diced fine
Fish Stock (for
   poaching, see
   page 156)
white wine (for
   poaching)
lettuce and tomato (for
   the plate)

2 tablespoons Dijon
   mustard
4½ cups oil (½ olive
   oil, ½ corn oil)
½ cup fresh chopped basil

In a food processor or blender, grind the scallops and fish at high speed until puréed.

Reduce to low speed and add the egg whites and eggs, the seasonings, and the cream.

Turn off the machine and incorporate the lobster meat by hand.

To cook, spoon the mixture out onto a few thicknesses of cheesecloth, about 2' by 1'.

Roll the mixture into a salami shape in the cloth, about 3" by 12". Tie off the ends.

Poach the "salami" in a combination (equal parts) of Fish Stock and white wine. Use enough liquid to cover. Place a meat thermometer in the center of the mousse, and barely simmer for about ¾ hour, or until the thermometer reads 150°. When done, allow it to cool in the stock.

Make the Basil Sauce: Combine the yolks, salt and pepper, vinegar, and mustard, and mix.

Beat in the oil, a bit at a time, as you would for a mayonnaise, until it is thick (though a little thinner than a commercial mayonnaise).

Stir in the chopped basil.

When the mousse is at room temperature, remove from the fluid, allow to drain, and remove the cheesecloth carefully.

Cut into ¼" slices and serve on a lettuce leaf, with a slice of tomato. Serve the sauce separately in a gooseneck sauceboat.

As a wine to go with this delicious appetizer, try a 1980 Côtes-du-Rhône Blanc from Hermitage Chante Alouette Chapoutier.

■■■■■■■■MARINATED SHRIMP■■■■■■ ■
BATON ROUGE (D.C.)

Enough for 6-8 servings

In order to get the full benefit of the terrific marinade, allow the shrimp to stand, refrigerated, for the full 12 hours called for—or more. Chef Marcel recommends large shrimp that run about 16 to the pound (weighed without heads). If you cannot find the Creole mustard called for, then country-style Dijon has much the same flavor.

It does not matter if the shrimp are not completely cooked through; the marinating completes the cooking.

SHRIMP:
3 pounds raw shrimp
½ gallon water

MARINADE:
⅓ cup wine vinegar
3 teaspoons Creole
** mustard**
½ cup olive oil
1 teaspoon paprika
1 teaspoon finely
** chopped parsley**
1 teaspoon finely
** chopped shallots**

1 cup wine vinegar
pinch cayenne pepper

1 cup finely chopped
** celery**
½ teaspoon finely
** chopped garlic**
salt and cayenne pepper
** to taste**

lettuce (for the plate)

Cooking the Shrimp: Bring the shrimp to a boil in the water, vinegar, and pepper, and cook for a few minutes. Remove and peel.

Make the Marinade: Add the vinegar to the mustard and mix; mix in the oil and paprika; add the herbs and beat with a whisk; add salt and cayenne to taste.

Mix together the shrimp and marinade, cover, and store refrigerated overnight, at least 12 hours. (I tossed the ingredients a few times during the marinating because the marinade did not cover the shrimp completely.)

Serve 6 to 8 shrimp per helping on a lettuce leaf.

With this spicy dish, you'll want a wine with personality: Try a California Chardonnay, such as the 1982 Alexander Valley Château Bouchaine.

SCALLOPS SAUTÉS FINES HERBES (D.C.)

Serves 2

Be sure to chop the herbs beforehand; you'll be too busy to chop once the scallops go into the sauté pan.

3 tablespoons sweet butter
1 pound fresh sea or bay scallops
1 tablespoon chopped fresh tarragon
1 tablespoon chopped fresh chives
1 tablespoon chopped fresh parsley
½ tablespoon chopped fresh basil
1 teaspoon chopped fresh mint
1 tablespoon chopped shallots
1 tablespoon lemon juice
salt and pepper

Brown the butter in a hot pan, add the scallops, and sear and shake, sear and shake, until they begin to shrink (they'll be about three-quarters cooked).

Add all the herbs and shallots, and again shake the pan to keep everything from sticking.

Add the lemon juice and salt and pepper to taste, and remove from the heat immediately.

With this dish, try a Rutherford Hill, Sauvignon Blanc, 1981, from California, or a Chablis, Grand Cru, Moreau, 1981.

■■■■SCALLOPS ORLÉANNAISE (D.C.) ■■■■ ■

Serves 2

Here is a dish as beautiful to serve as it is delicious to taste. *Fumet* is a light fish stock. The scallop shell called for is a pastry in the form of a large scallop shell, available at gourmet shops.

(Though bay scallops are called for, you can substitute sea scallops.)

1 pound fresh spinach (stems trimmed)	**½ cup white wine**
2 tablespoons sweet butter	**½ cup *Fumet* (see page 156)**
juice of ½ lemon	**½ cup Vin Blanc Sauce (see page 163)**
salt and pepper	**2 tablespoons Saffron Butter (see page 163)**
4 tablespoons chopped tomato, peeled and seeded	**2 pastry scallop shells**
1 pound bay scallops	

Sauté the spinach in butter, with lemon juice and salt and pepper, until barely softened (do not overcook). Reserve and keep warm.

Heat the tomatoes. Reserve and keep warm.

Poach the scallops at a simmer in white wine and *Fumet* until half done—30 seconds for bay scallops (1 full minute if you use sea scallops instead).

Remove the scallops and set aside. Reduce the poaching liquid until it is very thick, then add the Vin Blanc Sauce.

Bring to the boil and whip in the Saffron Butter, then add the scallops and heat briefly, but do not boil.

Rim 2 plates with the spinach (as shown in the photo on page 84), leaving space for the pastry shell at one end. Set the pastry shells in the spaces and spoon half the scallops onto each shell. Spoon the tomatoes between the spinach and the shell.

For this dish, a dry Sancerre is recommended, such as Clos de la Crele, Domain Lucien, 1982.

■■■■■■BAKED CLAMS CASINO (D.C.)■■■■ ■

Serves 3 (6 clams each)

Here is a traditional baked-clam dish, usually served as an appetizer, but with enough body to be a light main course. All the vegetables in this recipe should be chopped *quite* fine.

½ **pound sweet butter**
1 **large shallot, chopped**
¼ **teaspoon chopped**
garlic
⅓ **green pepper,**
chopped
⅔ **red pepper,**
chopped

1½ **tablespoons**
chopped parsley
1½ **tablespoons brandy**
salt and pepper
18 **one-inch bits of raw bacon**
18 **clams**

Allow the butter to soften to room temperature.

Chop all the vegetables fine, and mix well into the butter.

Add the brandy and stir in, then taste for salt and pepper.

Open each clam, and drain. Cut all the flesh and membranes free, scraping all the meat of each clam onto one of its half-shells.

Spread about a tablespoon of the butter mixture over each clam, and place on a baking tray. (The tray needs sides—the butter will melt and drip.)

Place a bit of bacon slice on each clam, over the butter.

Broil until the bacon is crisp and the butter bubbles—about 9 or 10 minutes.

Serve on a heatproof dish (6 clams per serving), with the melted butter spooned back over the clams.

■■■■■COLD LOBSTER PARISIENNE (N.Y.)■■■■ ■

Serves 1

Here is a cold dish sure to bring a glow to the eyes of anyone who likes food beautifully plated. Once you have the parts assembled, it should take you less time to put the dish together than it will to read about it.

COURT-BOUILLON (For Boiling):

3 quarts water
½ medium onion, sliced
½ medium carrot, sliced
a few sprigs of fresh parsley

a sprig of fresh thyme
1 bay leaf
½ cup vinegar
salt, to taste
a few peppercorns

LOBSTER:

1 fresh lobster, 1½ pounds
total of 1 cup cooked and diced vegetables (carrots, turnips, potatoes, green beans, peas)

Mayonnaise, to taste (see page 161)
bibb lettuce (for the plate)

Boiling: Combine the ingredients of the Court-Bouillon and bring to the boil.

Add the lobster, and cook for about 11 minutes, then turn off the heat and allow to cool for about 20 minutes in the bouillon.

The Lobster: Separate the head and tail sections. Remove the meat from the tail and split it in half lengthwise, and devein it. Set it aside. Remove the tail fins, split these shells into two small fans, and reserve for decoration. Discard the rest of the tail shell.

Remove the innards from the head half, and discard them. Remove the large claws, and separate the meat from the shells (discard the shells).

Remove and reserve the 6 largest side claws.

Plating: Place the empty head section of the shell on the plate so that it faces you, right side up, near the rim. Place the small claws so that they overlap (see photo, page 77).

Mix the vegetables with a little Mayonnaise. (Make certain the vegetables are well drained before you mix them with the Mayonnaise—there should be no fluid on the plate.)

Place a few leaves of bibb lettuce on the plate, behind the head section. The first leaf should overlap the shell.

Place the vegetables on the lettuce leaf behind the head.

Place the meat from the large claws so that they overlap the small claws and frame the vegetables.

Place the two sections of tail meat so that they curl around like a pair of ram's horns, one end of each tail section near one end of each of the large claws.

Finally, take the tail fins (separated into two sections) and place them flat, to cover the place where the tail meat and the claw meat come together.

I wouldn't want to tackle this delightful dish without Bill Pell's excellent photo.

▪ FOWL ▪

▪■■■■■■CHICKEN HASH (N.Y.)■■■■■■▪

Serves 2

This simple recipe is a very popular choice among Jockey Club regulars.

**2 chicken breasts,
 ground
1 shallot, chopped
1 tablespoon sweet
 butter
1 cup heavy cream
salt and pepper**

**sherry
1 tablespoon Chicken
 Velouté (optional, see
 page 143)
½ teaspoon finely
 chopped black truffle**

Sauté the ground chicken breasts and the chopped shallot in butter until golden.

Stir in 1 cup of cream, salt and pepper, and a splash of sherry. (To thicken the mixture slightly, you may here stir in an optional tablespoon of Chicken Velouté.)

Cook, uncovered, for 5-8 minutes over a low flame.

Just before serving, mix in the chopped black truffle.

Sommelier John Benevento recommends a 1981 Beaujolais, Cru Morgan by Fessy, as appropriate for this dish.

Lobster Ravioli in Champagne Sauce

Cappelleti in Tomato Sauce

■■■■CORNISH HEN À-LA-DIABLE (D.C.)■■■ ■

Serves 2

If you lack a grill, the bird may be seared in a frying pan with a little oil.

This recipe works equally well with a Cornish hen or with a 1½- to 2-pound chicken—in which case we call it *Poulet à-la-Diable.*

You can expect any dish with "devil" in its name to be either sharp (vinegar) or hot (pepper). This piquant sauce is both sharp and hot —but not overwhelmingly so.

HEN:
1 Cornish hen   **bread crumbs**
corn oil

SAUCE DIABLE:
1½ cups wine vinegar   **½ teaspoon chopped**
½ cup white wine   **tarragon**
1 teaspoon chopped fresh   **1 egg yolk**
parsley   **2 tablespoons sweet**
½ teaspoon crushed   **butter, at room**
peppercorns   **temperature**

GARNISH:
French sour pickle,   **chopped parsley**
julienne

The Hen: Split the hen in half lengthwise, down through the center of the back and breastbone.

Dip it lightly in corn oil, then in fresh bread crumbs. (Fresh bread can be crumbed in your blender.)

Sear the halves on a hot grill for 1 minute each side, then put into the oven and broil for 20 minutes.

Make the Sauce Diable: Combine the vinegar, wine, parsley, crushed peppercorns (peppercorns can be prepared easily and quickly by placing them on a bit of parchment, then crushing them with the bottom of a heavy pot), and tarragon in a pan and cook slowly until very little liquid remains.

Stir in the egg yolk, and when mixed, add the butter, a bit at a time, stirring constantly. (The butter must be at room temperature. This *beurre pommade* gives the sauce a velvety finish.) Once the butter is in, remove from the heat.

Before serving, beat the sauce a bit until it thickens.

Serve the hen with a light coating of the sauce and a garnish of chopped parsley and a fine julienne of imported French pickle.

With this spicy dish you will enjoy a white Burgundy, such as the 1981 Chablis Grand-Cru from Les Clos Moreau.

■━━━━ROAST SPRING CHICKEN WITH━━━■ ■
ASPARAGUS BUTTER (D.C.)

Serves 4 for lunch

This Asparagus Butter is arguably the best sauce I've ever tasted for chicken. The flavor is delicate, but still definite enough to have character—and not overshadow the chicken.

Though a very small bird is called for, any size bird could be used.

CHICKEN:
1 young chicken (1½-2 pounds)
1 tablespoon olive oil
salt and pepper

up to 4 tablespoons sweet butter (optional, for basting)

STUFFING:
1 carrot, diced
1 celery stalk, diced
½ medium onion, diced

pinch thyme
½ teaspoon fresh ground pepper

DEGLAZING:
1 ounce Madeira

1 ounce Armagnac

ASPARAGUS BUTTER:
10-12 stalks asparagus
cooking water (or Chicken Stock, see page 155)

1 cup heavy cream
salt and pepper
¼ pound butter, at room temperature

Preheat your oven to 375°.

Rub the outside of the chicken with olive oil, and sprinkle with salt and pepper.

Mix the Stuffing ingredients together (diced vegetables, thyme and pepper), and stuff the bird.

Roast at 375° for 35-40 minutes (or more, if needed), until golden brown, basting with the chicken fat as it melts out. If there is not enough fat with which to baste, you can add up to 4 tablespoons of butter, melting it in the roasting pan.

Plating: even a simple veal chop becomes special
with imaginative placement of vegetable garnish

Cold buffet: your basic simple lobster and asparagus

When cooked, remove the chicken, hold it above the pan, and pour out the contents of the body cavity: the chicken juices and the vegetables. Put the chicken aside.

Now, drain the fat off the chicken juices, and, with a slotted spoon, remove and discard the vegetables. This leaves only the chicken juices in the roasting pan. (Theoretically, the vegetables are discarded because they have given their all to the chicken in cooking; actually, I find them quite tasty and exercise the cook's privilege of snacking on them while I prepare the Asparagus Butter.)

Deglaze the roasting pan by adding an ounce each of Madeira (*real* Madeira) wine and Armagnac brandy, and scraping the brown bits into the liquid. Cook on top of the stove until the liquid gets syrupy.

Make the Asparagus Butter: Meanwhile, cut the bottom 2″ of stem off the asparagus (these ends are discarded), and peel. Steam the asparagus over plain water (or boil the asparagus in Chicken Stock, if you have it) until quite soft. Then grind them to a fine paste in a blender or food processor.

Add the asparagus paste to the deglazing liquid and mix.

Add the cream and cook over low heat until the texture gets creamy.

Pass the mixture through a fine sieve, and taste for the addition of salt and pepper.

Over very low heat, add the butter a bit at a time, stirring. The sauce must not boil during the addition of the butter, or after the butter is in.

Quarter the chicken when the sauce is ready, and serve each quarter covered with Asparagus Butter.

Garnish with medium egg noodles or plain white rice.

With this dish, Chef Marcel recommends an Alastian Gewürztraminer, such as the Trimbach, 1981.

■■■■■DUCK BREAST WITH RASPBERRY ■■■■ ■
SAUCE AND WILD RICE (D.C.)

Serves 4

Both sides from 1 duck (2 pieces) make up 1 breast.

When you prepare this dish, the wild rice should be started first, then the sauce, then the duck.

WILD RICE:
1 cup wild rice
1 quart light Chicken
  Stock (see
  page 155)

½ cup chopped pecans
¼ cup diced cooked
  goose liver
salt and pepper

RASPBERRY SAUCE:
2 tablespoons sugar
4 ounces raspberry
  vinegar
1 pint fresh raspberries
2½ cups Duck Stock
  (see page 158)

1 tablespoon arrowroot
  starch (dissolved in
  water)
salt and pepper

DUCK:
4 skinless boneless duck
  breasts
2 tablespoons olive oil

fresh raspberries (for
  garnish)

Cook 1 cup of wild rice in Chicken Stock until tender. (A "light" stock is called for; if your Chicken Stock is quite rich, dilute it by a quarter.) When the wild rice is done, strain, and add the pecans and chopped liver; stir, and taste for salt and pepper. Meanwhile, begin the sauce.

Raspberry Sauce: Combine the sugar, the vinegar, and a pint of raspberries, and, over a medium flame, reduce until syrupy.

Add the Duck Stock and cook slowly for an additional 15 minutes.

Allow to cool briefly, then purée in a blender or food processor. Strain to get rid of the seeds, and then return to the stove over a medium flame.

Stir in the arrowroot starch dissolved in a little bit of cold water. Continue to cook briefly, and then taste for salt and pepper.

As the sauce nears the finish, sauté the breasts in hot oil, about 5 minutes per side, until medium done.

Slice each breast, and spread the slices into a fan shape on each plate; garnish with fresh raspberries, then coat with the sauce.

Noisettes of Venison Grand Veneur, with Chestnut Purée

Entrance to the N.Y. Jockey Club.
Understatement on Central Park South

■━━━━━━━DUCK TERRINE (N.Y.)━━━━━■ ■
Terrine de Canard

Yields about 20 slices

This recipe for a country-style appetizer is started the day before. "Terrine" is the name of the earthenware dish in which a terrine is cooked.

The pork fat called for is thin to begin with and must be sliced even thinner. Chef Daniel says a mechanical slicer is fine, but if you use a knife, he warns, be careful not to cut yourself.

We cook this recipe with its cover on. But while it is cooling, the cover is removed and replaced with a clean wooden board, to compress the terrine.

1 duck (including its liver)	**½ cup Duck Stock, reduced to 3 tablespoons (see page 158)**
4 ounces cognac	**pinch thyme**
1 pound pork shoulder	**2 bay leaves, crumbled**
10 ounces pork back fat	**pepper**
½ an apple, peeled	**a few pistachio nuts**
1 shallot, chopped	**thin strips of pork back fat (to cover the sides and bottom of the terrine)**
1 pound mushrooms	
½ pound additional duck livers or chicken livers	
½ cup Madeira	
4 teaspoons salt	

First Day: Skin and bone the duck (or have your butcher do it for you), keeping the skin in one piece (reserve the carcass for the stock).

Remove the breast, cut it into strips, and marinate it in cognac overnight.

Second Day: Preheat your oven to 350°.

Keeping the breast meat aside, grind the remaining duck with the pork shoulder, back fat, apple, shallot, mushrooms, and all the livers.

Into the same ground mixture, stir in the cognac in which the breast strips have been marinating, the Madeira, salt, Duck Stock, seasonings, and pistachios.

Garnish the bottom and sides of a terrine mold with thin strips of pork fat.

Press a layer of the mixture into the terrine, arrange the strips of breast over the surface, then fill up with the rest of the mixture.

Top with more thin slices of pork back fat or with the duck skin.

Cover. Set the terrine in a pan with 1 cup of hot water, and bake for 1½ hours in a 350° oven.

When done, remove from the oven, take off the cover, and cover with a wooden board, held down with a light weight.

Serve when cool, 1 slice per person.

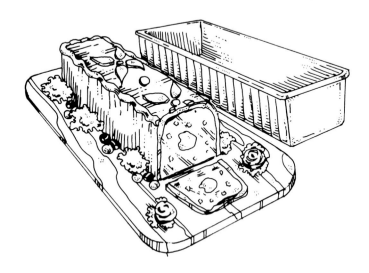

■ ■■■■■■■SAUTÉED GOOSE LIVER (D.C.)■■■■■■ ■

Serves 1

I am not a liver lover, but I tasted this dish on the recommendation of Eric Ewoldt (vice-president and managing director of the D.C. Ritz-Carlton), and it changed my mind. This is so good.

A fresh, raw goose liver should run about 1½ pounds; a serving should be 2½ to 3 ounces of ⅛″ slices. The number of slices in an individual serving will, of course, vary, depending on the thickness of the liver where you take the slice. Now that I've cleared that up . . . .

If you keep Demiglace only for this recipe, it is worth the trouble.

raw fresh goose liver
(2½ to 3 ounces)
1 tablespoon clarified
butter
3 tablespoons Marsala or
Madeira
3 seedless red grapes,
halved

3 seedless green grapes,
halved
3 tablespoons Demiglace
(see page 162)
salt and pepper
(optional)

Slice the liver in ⅛" slices.

Sauté the liver very briefly in clarified butter—*a few seconds per side*. Though sliced thin, it is still to be pink in the middle. When it is cooked, remove it from the pan and set it aside in a place where it will stay warm but will not cook further.

Discard most of the butter, and deglaze with about 3 tablespoons of a good quality Marsala or Madeira. Add the grape halves, and reduce the liquid until almost dry.

Stir in 3 tablespoons of Demiglace, bring to the boil, then remove from the heat. Taste for the possible addition of salt and pepper. It will usually need nothing.

Pour over the liver slices.

Serve with French bread, or with toast.

Entrance to the D.C. Ritz-Carlton, on the corner of
Massachusetts Avenue and 21st Street

▪ GAME ▪

Game dishes are not to everyone's palate. Some complain that they are too ... gamy. Game dishes are often marinated, to tame this "wild" flavor.

▪ ▬▬▬▬▬BREAST OF MALLARD IN ▬▬▬▬▬ ▪ PORT WINE SAUCE (N.Y.)

Each breast serves 1

Mallard ducks, familiar sights to us, are considered a delicacy in France.

breast of 1 mallard
salt and pepper
2 tablespoons butter
4 ounces port wine
Veal Stock (see
page 157)

1 teaspoon arrowroot
starch
2 tablespoons port

Remove the breast of the mallard, leaving the skin on. Season on both sides with salt and pepper.

Melt the butter in a pan, and, when hot, put in the mallard breast.

Cook gently, covered, for about 5 minutes. The breast should be served quite pink.

When done, remove the breast and drain off and discard the fat.

Deglaze the pan with about 4 ounces of port wine and a little Veal Stock (that is, pour the wine and Veal Stock into the pan and scrape into it the bits of mallard sticking to the sides and bottom).

Mix a little arrowroot starch into a couple of additional tablespoons of port, stir into the pan, and heat a bit until slightly thickened. This is your sauce.

Remove the skin and slice the breast into a fan shape.

Put the sauce on the dish and arrange the breast on top.

With this tasty dish, a Côtes-du-Rhône would be appropriate, such as the Châteauneuf-du-Pape by Château la Gardine.

■■■■■■■BOAR TENDERLOIN (D.C.)■■■■■ ■
Filet de Marcassin à la Crème

Serves about 20

The ingredients in the Marinade are for 4 filets of boar tenderloin, 2½ pounds each.

MARINADE:

1 gallon red wine	2 medium carrots, sliced
1 medium onion, sliced	1 teaspoon thyme
¼ of a whole celery, chopped	2-3 bay leaves
4 cloves garlic, crushed	2 cloves
½ cup chopped parsley stems	

4 tenderloins of boar (about 2½ pounds each)	6 tablespoons sweet butter, at room temperature
¼ cup corn oil	4 teaspoons currant jelly
5 ounces cognac	
2 pints heavy cream	
fresh-ground pepper	

Combine the ingredients of the Marinade, and marinate the meat for 2 or 3 days.

Drain off the fluid, reserve the vegetables, and allow the meat to drain on a towel for 3-4 hours.

Preheat the oven to 400°.

Heat the oil in a pan large enough for all the meat. Put in the meat and the vegetables, and sear the tenderloins on both sides. Put into a 400° oven and cook for 20-30 minutes, until a meat thermometer registers 118°-120° (for medium rare).

Remove the pan from the oven, and reserve the tenderloins.

Skim off the fat, and deglaze the pan with the cognac, scraping the bits from the sides and bottom into the mixture.

Add 2 pints cream and allow to reduce about a quarter.

Sprinkle with fresh-ground pepper.

Thicken with room-temperature butter, stirring in a bit at a time. Don't allow the sauce to boil after the butter is in.

Finish by stirring the currant jelly into the sauce.

Put some sauce on the plate, and lay a couple of slices of tenderloin over that. Serve the rest of the sauce on the side in a cruet.

Garnish with Braised Celery (see page 54) and Chestnut Purée (see page 54).

With this flavorful dish, try a wine from my favorite part of France, the Côte-d'Or; Nuits-Saint-Georges, Les Richmones Moillard, 1978.

■ ■■■■■RABBIT IN MUSTARD SAUCE (D.C.)■■■■ ■
Lapin Sauté Morvandelle

Serves 4

The rabbit called for is not wild but domestic, and, so, more tender and delicate of flavor. Cut it into 8 pieces (or have your butcher cut it) as follows: Remove the forelegs and hindlegs (do not joint them); cut the remaining carcass into 4 more-or-less equal segments, across the spine.

1 rabbit in 8 pieces	**½ cup diced smoked**
½ cup corn oil	**bacon**
2 cups white wine	**a pinch of thyme**
⅓ cup Dijon mustard	**2 bay leaves**
½ cup peeled and seeded	**2 cups Chicken Stock**
tomatoes, chopped	**(see page 155)**
2 teaspoons chopped	**salt and pepper**
shallots	
1 teaspoon chopped	
garlic	

Preheat your oven to about 375°.

Brown the rabbit in hot corn oil, on all sides, then remove and set in a colander to drain.

Discard the fat, and deglaze the pan with 2 cups of white wine. When well stirred, allow it to reduce by half over a medium-high flame.

When reduced, lower the flame, add the remaining ingredients, and mix well. Allow to cook for 10 minutes. Taste for salt and pepper.

Add the rabbit, cover the dish, and bake at about 375° for 30-40 minutes.

Chef Marcel suggests a Gevrey-Chambertin, Laboure Roi, 1979; Bill Kennedy opts for a light-bodied red Bordeaux, such as a Pomerol.

PHEASANT PÂTÉ (N.Y.)
Pâté de Faisan en Croûte

As an appetizer, yields enough for a large dinner party

Here is a recipe in the grand tradition—and the first dish I ever tasted at the New York Jockey Club. It told me I was on to a good thing.

Both the crust and the pâté are started 24 hours in advance, and then the finished pâté should be refrigerated overnight before serving cold. You can also make the Pheasant Stock the first day. Pheasant Stock is made like Duck Stock (see recipe on page 158) but with pheasant bones.

The pheasant leg meat is ground, but the breasts are kept whole and marinated.

The recipe requires a rectangular pâté mold.

CRUST:

3 cups flour
6 tablespoons sweet
  butter

2 teaspoons salt
tepid water

PÂTÉ:

meat from 2 pheasants,
  boned (should include
  about 12 ounces from
  legs)
salt and pepper
Madeira wine
1 cup heavy cream
8 ounces pork back fat
2 tablespoons Pheasant
  Stock (made from the
  pheasant bones)

1 scant ounce truffles,
  chopped fine
2 ounces good cognac
butter (for mold)
additional pork back fat
  (to top the pâté)
1 egg yolk (for glaze)

ASPIC:

2 tablespoons butter
½ carrot, diced
½ onion, diced
1 stalk celery, diced
2 cups water
2 cups white wine

salt and pepper
bay leaf
pinch thyme
2 juniper berries
½ packet gelatin
2 ounces Madeira

MADEIRA GAME SAUCE (optional):

1 cup stock
¼ tablespoon chopped
  truffles

½ cup Madeira
½ cup Demiglace
  (see page 162)

Prepare the Crust: Put the flour into a large bowl and shape into a well. Work the butter and salt into a smooth paste, then work into the flour.

Add warm water a little at a time, working until the dough is firm. (Chef Daniel says the amount of water will vary from day to day.)

Cover with a cloth overnight.

The Pâté Itself: Take the 2 pheasant breasts, cut them in half, put them into a dish, season with salt and pepper, barely cover with Madeira, and put aside for 24 hours.

Remove the veins and ligaments from the leg meat, grind it very fine, and put the meat into a bowl.

Slowly add the cream, and some salt and pepper.

Grind the half pound of pork back fat very fine and add it to the mixture.

Mix in the Pheasant Stock.

Pass the mixture through a fine sieve.

Add the chopped truffles and the cognac, mix well, and refrigerate for 24 hours.

Second Day: Preheat your oven to 350°.

Rub the inside of a pâté mold with butter.

Roll out thin about 80% of the dough, and line the mold, leaving a ½" of dough flopping down outside the mold. (You reserve the rest of the dough to cover the mold later.)

At the bottom put in a 1" layer of the ground meat mixture, and over this a layer of the pheasant breast; then another layer of each, finishing with a layer of the ground meat.

Cover the top layer with a thin strip of pork back fat.

Wet the ½" of dough that flops over the top of the mold.

Roll out a strip of dough to cover the top of the mold: Cut it to the size of the top with scissors.

Lay the strip on top, fold over the moistened extra ½", and pinch hard together to really close off the pastry.

With scissors, snip 3 small holes down the center of the top; roll three small pieces of aluminum foil into "chimneys," and fit them into the holes. (This allows the hot air to escape without damaging the top crust.)

Glaze the top with a little scrambled egg yolk, brushed on with a pastry brush.

Bake at 350° for 1½ hours.

Make the Aspic: Melt the butter in a pan and sauté the vegetables until brown; add the water, wine, seasonings, and juniper berries; cook, simmering, for 1 hour. (This is actually a stock.)

Dissolve the gelatin in 2 cups of this stock and 2 ounces of Madeira wine.

Cold Pâté: Remove the cooked pâté from the oven and, while it is still warm, take out the "chimneys." Using a funnel, pour some Aspic through the holes until the mold is full. Adding the Aspic, or jelly, this way allows it to permeate the pâté. There is nothing better than permeated pâté.

Serve cold the next day.

Or Hot Pâté: To serve hot, the same day, finish with a Madeira Game Sauce instead of the Aspic. Simply take 1 cup of the same stock you were going to prepare for the Aspic (but without gelatin), reduce it by half. Add the truffles. Reduce ½ cup of Madeira by half (in a separate saucepan) and add it. Mix in ½ cup of Demiglace.

Serve over slices of the pâté.

NOISETTES OF VENISON GRAND VENEUR (N.Y.)

Serves 3

To serve 3 people, you will want 6 *noisettes* of venison loin—4 ounces per cut, 8 ounces per serving. As with much game, we start out with a marinade.

MARINADE:

2 tablespoons olive oil
1 small carrot, diced small
1 medium onion, diced small
1½ large shallots, chopped small
1 medium clove garlic, chopped small
6 sprigs parsley

6 sprigs thyme
6 peppercorns
2 cloves
6 juniper berries
2 teaspoons basil
2 teaspoons sage
1 quart white wine
1 cup wine vinegar

6 four-ounce loin *noisettes* of venison

POIVRADE SAUCE:

2 tablespoons sweet butter
2 tablespoons olive oil
1 carrot, diced
½ onion, diced
2 tablespoons diced celery
2 broken venison bones
venison trimmings

10 ounces vinegar
10 ounces white wine
2 quarts Game Stock (see page 158)
2 quarts Espagnole Sauce (see page 162)
additional Game Stock
Marinade

GRAND VENEUR SAUCE:

2 cups Poivrade Sauce
2 cups Game Stock
4 tablespoons red currant jelly

5 ounces heavy cream
salt and pepper

1 tablespoon butter

1 tablespoon olive oil

Marinade: Put the oil into a large pan and add all the vegetables and aromatics. Cook over a low flame until lightly colored.

Add the wine and vinegar and cook over a low flame for about 45 minutes. Allow to come to room temperature.

Marinate the venison in this mixture for 1 to 2 days.

Prepare the Poivrade Sauce: Put 2 tablespoons of butter and 2 table-spoons of oil in a large pot with a heavy bottom. Add the diced carrot, onion, and celery. Add some broken-up venison bones and venison trimmings, and cook over a low flame until well browned.

When browned, drain off and discard the grease, and add the vinegar and white wine.

Reduce by three-quarters.

Add 2 quarts of Game Stock and 2 quarts of Espagnole Sauce. Cover, bring to the boil, then put into a moderate oven (about 375°) for 3 hours.

When done, strain (press the fluid out of the solids), and pour into a pan.

Thin with additional Game Stock and Marinade in equal portions until the sauce is *nappé* (will coat a wooden spoon).

Make the Grand Veneur Sauce: To 2 cups of Poivrade Sauce, add 2 cups of Game Stock, then reduce by a third; when reduced, stir in the jelly and cream. Season with salt and pepper.

Cook the Venison: We come now to the climax of this exercise in *la grande cuisine*—or anticlimax—the brief cooking of the venison.

Heat the butter and oil in a pan. When quite hot, add your venison. Cook about 3 minutes per side—after all, it has been marinating at least a day.

Serve with the Grand Veneur Sauce poured over the *noisettes.* Chef Daniel recommends Chestnut Purée as a side dish (recipe on page 54).

With this spectacular creation, try a Côtes-du-Rhône, such as a Châteauneuf-du-Pape "Château Rayas" by Reynaud.

▪ PASTA ▪

Pasta Sauces

There is a great deal of pasta served at the New York Jockey Club. In fact, a *pasta du jour* is always featured. Usually, this pasta feature is Linguini, and the Jockey Club presents a different sauce daily, but all are based on a cream sauce. The recipe for the Linguini itself follows after this group of cream sauces.

■ ━━━━━━CHICKEN SAUCE (N.Y.)━━━━━━ ■

Serves 4

Here is the basic recipe, using chicken, but it can be adapted in many different ways.

Velouté means "velvety," and that is how dishes turn out when you use it. You'll notice that the Chicken Velouté we use here is just a *roux* (a mixture of melted butter and flour) with Chicken Stock added. Chicken Velouté is quite thick and creamy—it should have no lumps.

2 cups heavy cream	pinch of saffron
white of 1 large leek	1 cup Chicken Velouté
1 cup raw chicken breast	salt and pepper
1 tablespoon sweet butter	

CHICKEN VELOUTÉ:

2 tablespoons sweet butter	1 cup Chicken Stock (see page 155)
3 tablespoons flour	

Reduce the heavy cream by a quarter by simmering it over a low flame.

Shred the white of the leek and the chicken into fine pieces and sauté them in a little butter until just golden. Add the reduced cream and a pinch of saffron, and stir together.

Make the Chicken Velouté: Melt 2 tablespoons of butter, and, over a medium flame, mix in 3 tablespoons of flour, and 1 cup of Chicken Stock, stirring for a minute or so, until the mixture is thick and velvety.

Add the velouté to the cream-and-leek-and-chicken mixture and stir until it is satisfactorily creamy. It should have body, and it should stick well to the pasta, but it should not be gummy.

Salt and pepper to taste.

Fold the sauce into the Linguini. Or, you might want to heap the Linguini onto an individual serving dish, make a "nest" in the center with the back of a spoon, and pour the sauce into the nest.

■■■■FISH OR SCALLOPS SAUCE (N.Y.)■■■■

Serves 4

To make your pasta sauce with fish or scallops, substitute 1 cup of fish or scallops for the chicken, and make a Fish Velouté with Fish Stock (recipe on page 156), or with white wine if you have no Fish Stock. (What? You mean that you don't keep Fish Stock on hand in your refrigerator, just in case?)

Otherwise, proceed as you do in the Chicken Sauce recipe just preceding.

Serves 4

This is similar to the Chicken Sauce, but just different enough to make for trouble, so I'll give you the recipe from scratch.

2 cups heavy cream	**pinch of curry powder**
white of 1 large leek	**1 cup Fish Velouté**
1 cup raw baby shrimp, peeled	**salt and pepper**
1 tablespoon sweet butter	

FISH VELOUTE:

2 tablespoons sweet butter	**1 cup Fish Stock (see page 156) or dry white wine**
3 tablespoons flour	

Reduce the cream by about a quarter.

Shred the leek, add to it the baby shrimp *(whole, not shredded)*, and sauté them in the butter until golden.

Add the reduced cream and a pinch of curry powder, and stir together.

Make the Fish Velouté: Melt the butter, and, over this same medium flame, mix the flour into the butter until smooth; then add the Fish Stock (or white wine) and continue to stir until thickened and smooth.

Mix together 1 cup of Fish Velouté and the shrimp combination, and stir until creamy.

Taste for the possible addition of salt and pepper.

Stir the sauce into the Linguini or serve in a "nest." (Heap the pasta onto an individual serving plate, and make a depression in the top of the heap with the back of a ladle—pour some sauce into the nest.)

■■■■SWEETBREADS AND MUSHROOMS■■■■
SAUCE (N.Y.)

Serves 4

This was the entrée at my first lunch at the Jockey Club. It knocked my socks off.

The Jockey Club will also serve any of the pastas as an appetizer. As a main course it serves 4, as an appetizer, 6 to 8.

Please do note that the sweetbreads must be started the day before with 24 hours of soaking.

2 sweetbreads
sweet butter
½ cup diced celery
½ cup diced carrots
½ cup diced onion
pinch thyme
1 bay leaf
1 cup Veal Stock (see
    page 157)
1 cup white wine
1 cup cleaned and
    quartered mushrooms
a few shallots
2 cups heavy cream
chopped fresh basil
    (for garnish)
chopped fresh parsley
    (for garnish)

Soak the sweetbreads in cold water for 24 hours.

Preheat your oven to 300°-350°.

Blanch the sweetbreads (that is, put them into boiling water and boil for 2 minutes), remove them from the water, and clean them under cold running water. To clean, remove the outer covering, the veins, and anything else that doesn't look white.

Braise them whole: Melt a little butter in a pan, put in the sweetbreads, and add the celery, carrots, onion, thyme, and a bay leaf.

Cook a short while, covered, over a medium flame, then turn over and continue cooking.

When golden, add the Veal Stock and white wine to the pan.

Put into a 300°-350° oven, and cook, covered, until tender—about ½ to ¾ hour.

While the sweetbreads are cooking, prepare the mushrooms: Wipe them clean, quarter them, and sauté with a few finely chopped shallots in a little butter.

Add 2 cups of heavy cream to the mushrooms and cook briefly, until the cream is hot.

Remove the sweetbreads from the oven and slice into small pieces.

Drain off the liquid from the sweetbreads pan and add it to the cream and mushrooms, stirring, over a low flame.

Fold in the sweetbreads, still over a low flame, until heated. Garnish with chopped fresh basil and parsley.

■■■■■LINGUINI or FETTUCCINE (N.Y.)■■■■■

Yields 4 main-course helpings or 6-8 appetizer-course helpings

With a flattened pasta, such as Linguini, you get more sauce and less pasta per forkful.

Knowing that I was to work on this book, my wife and I bought a pasta-making machine and taught ourselves to use it. We found the fresh homemade pasta so superior that we gave away the boxes of commercial pasta in our closet. So, one reason we love the pastas we eat at the New York Jockey Club is not just the sauces—but the fresh-made Linguini and Fettuccine. Not that pasta doesn't dry marvelously well, but it's like discussing the difference between fresh and dried herbs.

Linguini (and Fettuccine—which uses the same proportions) is made in the basement of the New York Jockey Club, fresh daily— unless the pasta man is on vacation, in which case it can be stored for a day or two in the refrigerator, or it can be frozen for weeks. A pasta-making machine is used—a large Italian commercial model. I used the recipe in my home pasta-making machine, adjusting for the limits that my machine sets (it won't hold a full pound of flour). It worked fine.

Please do use the durham flour called for: It is harder than the all-purpose flour sold for baking, and maintains its integrity better when cooked.

This recipe calls for no salt in the pasta.

2⅔ cups (1 pound)	**3 or 4 eggs**
durham flour	

Put the flour into your pasta maker as called for in the machine's instructions. Mix in 3 eggs, and work for a few minutes. If the texture of the dough requires more fluid, put in another egg or a bit of water.

Work until ready to extrude.

Extrude the pasta, cutting it into 10″ to 12″ lengths.

Allow to dry briefly, then refrigerate until ready to use.

When ready to cook, boil about 6 quarts of lightly salted water per pound of pasta. Put the Linguini into boiling water, and allow the water to return to the boil. Start timing from this return. Start tasting after about 4 minutes of boiling. Yes, fresh-made pasta cooks up much faster than dry pasta.

CAPPELLETI WITH HERBS AND TOMATO (N.Y.)

Serves 8

These 1" filled pastas look like tiny hats: sailor caps with exaggerated brims all around, or perhaps a dunce cap with a brim—but with the point cut off and rounded.

Cappelleti are made of almost-paper-thin circles of dough with a bit of filling in the center; the circle is folded in half over the filling, forming a fat crescent-moon shape; the points of the crescent moon are then overlapped and pressed together. A bit of egg is used as the glue to hold all the foldings and pressings. Just follow the instructions below and you should have no trouble.

At the Jockey Club, they are served filled with a veal and pork combination, then covered with tomato sauce and fresh basil.

The spinach is blanched by tossing it into boiling water for 1 minute and then removing it. *It must be drained well.*

If you don't have a pasta maker, this dough can be kneaded and rolled out on a pastry board, but it must be rolled *very* thin, to the thickness of a few sheets of paper (that's not difficult with a dough this dry). If you do have a pasta maker with an adjustable thickness, set it for 1/32"—or just experiment.

The circles can be cut with a 2½" round cookie cutter.

Allow the cappelleti to dry in the refrigerator for several hours before cooking them.

PASTA:

4 cups durham flour

3 eggs

3 egg yolks

pinch of salt

FILLING:

2 tablespoons olive oil

1 tablespoon sweet
  butter

8 ounces lean veal,
  chopped

2 ounces prosciutto ham,
  chopped

3 ounces pork, chopped

1 clove garlic, chopped
  fine

1 sprig fresh rosemary

salt and pepper

3 ounces white wine

2 ounces fresh spinach,
  trimmed, blanched,
  chopped

1 egg

¼ cup grated Parmesan
  cheese

dash nutmeg

1 egg yolk (raw)

TOMATO SAUCE:

2 pounds ripe tomatoes

salt and pepper

2 tablespoons olive oil

1 small carrot, diced

1 small onion, diced

1 stalk celery, diced

3 ounces prosciutto,
  diced

6 fresh basil leaves,
  chopped

2 cloves garlic, chopped
  fine

1 tablespoon flour

2 bay leaves

sprig of fresh thyme

1 cup Chicken Stock
  (see page 155)

1 teaspoon sugar

salt and pepper (again)

2 tablespoons olive oil

chopped fresh basil
  (for garnish)

Making the Pasta: To make the pasta in a machine, combine the ingredients as per the machine instructions, but allow the machine to knead for several minutes. Extrude very thin. Flour your working surface, and cut into circles 2½" in diameter.

Alternatively, to make the pasta on a pastry board, mound the flour and shape a well in the center. Break the eggs and yolks into the well. Add the salt. Work the liquid ingredients into the flour to make a dough. When the dough is formed, knead for 5 minutes, then rest (you and the dough) for 20 minutes before rolling. Roll out paper thin, and cut into the same 2½" circles.

Making the Filling: Heat the oil and butter in a pan, and when hot, brown the veal, ham, and pork with the garlic, rosemary, and a little salt and pepper.

Add the white wine, and reduce by about half.

Cover the pan, lower the flame, and cook slowly for about 10 minutes.

Remove the cover and add the chopped spinach.

Whisk an egg and stir it in (to bind the mixture), then stir in the Parmesan cheese and a dash of nutmeg.

Making the Cappelleti: Take 1 of the raw pasta rounds and hold it in your left hand (if you are right-handed). Take a small pastry brush and dip it lightly into the egg yolk. Brush the egg yolk around the outside of half the pasta.

Take half a teaspoonful of filling and put it right onto the center of the pasta round.

Fold the pasta in half, bringing the unegged edge together with the egged edge. Press gently to seal it closed.

(Because of the filling, the half-made cappelleti now has the look of a fat crescent moon.)

Dip one tip of the folded pasta into a little bit of yolk. Now, bring the ends together, overlapping, and press the egged and unegged tips together to finish the cappelleti. Put onto a floured tray to hold.

To cook, drop into lightly salted boiling water for about 3 minutes, or until the pasta is tender. Remember, the filling is already cooked.

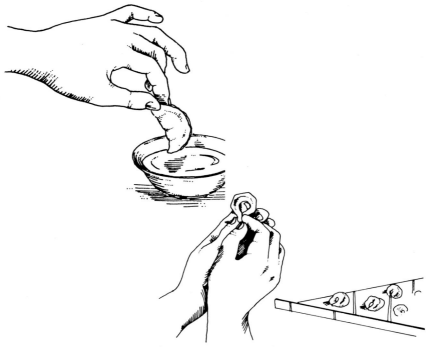

Making the Tomato Sauce: Peel, seed, and chop 2 pounds of ripe tomatoes. Sprinkle lightly with salt and pepper. Drain off any free fluid through a colander. Set the tomatoes aside.

Heat 2 tablespoons of oil in a pan, and cook the carrot, onion, celery, ham, basil, and garlic over a medium flame for a few minutes.

Sprinkle a tablespoon of flour over this mixture, and stir in. Cook for 2 minutes more.

Add the tomatoes, bay leaves, a sprig of fresh thyme, and the Chicken Stock. Stir together, and cook, covered, in a medium oven (about 375°) for about 1½ hours.

Remove from the oven. Strain the mixture to separate out all the fluids—this is your Tomato Sauce.

Sprinkle a teaspoon of sugar over the sauce, taste it for salt and pepper, and then stir in the remaining 2 tablespoons of olive oil.

To Serve: Drench the cappelleti with sauce, then serve sprinkled with chopped fresh basil.

RAVIOLI IN CHAMPAGNE
SAUCE (N.Y.)

Yields about 40 raviolis

The Jockey Club no longer makes its own ravioli pasta. Instead, it uses (hold on to your *toque*) egg-roll sheets—also known as egg-roll skins. And they work marvelously well.

So, I'll give no recipe here for the pasta itself. If your machine will roll out the dough thin enough—and yet uniform and strong enough—fine. Otherwise, egg-roll sheets it is. In my local supermarket, the egg-roll skins were $1.29 a pound, in the Oriental foods section.

The ravioli mold called for is an odd-looking object, with room to make a dozen raviolis at a time. It is an open gridwork with aluminum crosspieces about ⅜" across. A pasta sheet is laid across it. Raw egg (to act as glue to keep each ravioli together) is brushed on the pasta where the crosspieces are. Filling is put in the middle of each opening, and a second pasta sheet is laid on top. Then the whole thing is turned over and pressed onto the table—this closes the raviolis. The individual raviolis are then cut apart with a crimping wheel.

The ravioli can also be made without a mold. Place an egg-roll sheet on your board, and brush it lightly with egg yolk around the edges and across the middle, left to right, and up and down. Place your filling between these yolk "windows," then place another sheet over the first, and press down on the lines of egg yolk to seal. Then cut them apart with a crimping wheel. Quite simple, really, and no mold flipping to do.

FILLING:
½ pound raw lobster
  meat and lobster coral
salt and pepper
dash cayenne
1 egg white
1 cup heavy cream
1 teaspoon chopped
  truffles

PASTA:
egg-roll skins
1 egg yolk

Champagne Sauce (see
  page 91)

chopped truffles (for
  garnish)

Making the Filling: Grind the lobster and coral together until quite fine, then season with salt and pepper and a dash of cayenne pepper.

Pass it through a coarse sieve to make certain that it is chopped fine.

Put it into a bowl, and set the bowl in ice. Slowly and deliberately, whisk in the egg white, and then the cream. Beating the egg white and cream into the cold lobster mixture this way makes it thicken somewhat.

Stir in a teaspoon of chopped truffles.

Remove the bowl from the ice and refrigerate for 24 hours.

Making the Ravioli: Place a ravioli mold on your clean work surface. Put a sheet of pasta (or egg-roll sheet) onto the mold, and brush a little egg yolk onto the pasta where the mold supports it. (That egg yolk acts as glue to hold the pasta together.)

Place about 1½ teaspoons of filling on the center of each bit of pasta, where it sags down, between the supports.

Take another pasta sheet, and place it exactly over the first, pressing it down lightly on the supports.

Holding the mold by its ends, flip it over, and press it into your clean working surface. This pressure closes each Ravioli.

Remove the mold.

Cut the Ravioli apart with a crimping wheel, and set on a floured tray to hold until you are ready to cook them.

To cook, place your Ravioli in lightly salted boiling water, allow to come back to the boil, and cook for another 10 minutes. Unlike the Cappelleti filling (recipe on page 149), the Ravioli filling is raw, and so it must be cooked now.

Serve dipped in the hot Champagne Sauce. Garnish with some chopped truffles.

▪ SAUCES AND STOCKS ▪
BUILDING BLOCKS

Many of the recipes in this book require sauces and/or stocks. One of the characteristics of French cooking (and Continental cuisine in general) is that recipes are frequently built upon one another. You will need some Demiglace Sauce to make Tournedos Rossini (recipe on page 75), but you will need Sauce Espagnole to make the Demiglace, and you will need Veal Stock to make the Sauce Espagnole. (All the recipes are here.)

It sounds more complicated than it is. Most of the sauces and stocks can be made when time permits and then held in the refrigerator for a couple of weeks, or until you want to use them. (I keep jars of stocks in my fridge routinely—they come in handy for so many things, and I just don't want to have to spend a couple of hours making a stock before I can begin a recipe.)

The recipes for stocks are very flexible: A bit more of this or less of that will make little difference. After all, these are ingredients we are making, not finished dishes. However, when a lot of stock is used in a recipe, of course the flavor of the stock will seriously affect the flavor of the dish. Still, when you taste your stock for final seasoning, do keep in mind that if you salt your stock a lot, it gets saltier and saltier as it is reduced. It is easier to add salt than to take it out. A stock is not supposed to taste like a finished soup.

On the other hand, sauces should be made pretty much as the recipes indicate.

This is not to say that I am presenting here the one and only perfect way to make each sauce. Far from it. As one of the American-trained chefs I spoke to said, describing his experiences while training at the Culinary Institute of America: after studying under 18 chefs, he came away with 18 different (and all workable and good) methods for making Hollandaise! These sauces are practical recipes from men who make them (or supervise their making) daily.

Stocks

These are the workhorses of basic cooking. Stocks are generally simple to make. And, if you have the space and the plastic containers, they will freeze and store very well.

■━━━━━CHICKEN STOCK (N.Y.)━━━━━■

Yields about 2 quarts — but that will depend on the size of your pot

This is the recipe of Sous-Chef Rich Mikolitch. He prefers not to salt his stock, leaving salting for the final recipe. Backs are about the fattiest part of the chicken; do be certain to get rid of all the fat after cooking. If you have trouble skimming off the fat, store the stock with the fat, then remove from the refrigerator the next day and scoop off all the fat that has risen to the top and solidified.

**5 pounds chicken necks
  and backs
1 large onion, chopped
2 stalks celery, cleaned
  and chopped**

**1 carrot, chopped
1 bay leaf
water**

Into a large pot, put the chicken, onion, celery, carrot, and bay leaf. Then add water until it is about 1″ above the other ingredients.

Bring to the boil, and skim the scum off the surface.

Reduce to a simmer and cook, simmering, for about 2 hours. Continue to skim as the stock cooks. Skim off any fat that remains at the end of cooking.

When cooked, strain out the solids (and discard), and refrigerate the stock.

■━━━━━BEEF STOCK (N.Y.)━━━━━■

Yields about 1 gallon

Again, please note that Sous-Chef Rich has not included salt. Your cooking time can be reduced by an hour or so if you split the shin bones, but it is not necessary.

5 pounds beef shin bones	5 carrots, chopped
3 large onions, chopped	1 bay leaf
½ bunch celery, washed and chopped	water

Put all the solid ingredients in a very large pot and add 2½ gallons of water.

Bring to the boil, and skim off the scum.

Reduce to a simmer and cook, simmering for 6 hours, skimming as you cook.

There will be less fat to remove from this stock than there was in the Chicken Stock, but there will be more scum.

When cooked, remove from the heat, give a final skim, and strain to separate the solids (discard or give them to the dog) and the fluid (refrigerate).

■━━━━━FISH STOCK (N.Y.)━━━━━■
Fumet

In some of the recipes, a *Fumet* is called for instead of a Fish Stock. Generally speaking, *fumet* is lighter stuff, with just a *flavor* of the fish, as opposed to a rich stock. In this recipe, Chef Daniel Dunas gives us a light Fish Stock—which will serve as either stock or *fumet*.

2 tablespoons sweet butter	1 small leek, sliced
½ pound fish bones and heads (Dover sole preferred)	*bouquet garni*
	juice of 1 lemon
	6 whole peppercorns
a few mushrooms, sliced	dash salt
1 carrot, sliced	1 cup dry white wine
½ onion, sliced	1 quart cold water

BOUQUET GARNI:	
a sprig of parsley	(tie up with a bit of
a sprig of fresh thyme	string)
a bay leaf	

Melt the butter in the bottom of your stockpot.

Into the pot put the fish heads and bones, the mushrooms, the carrot, the onion, the leek, the *bouquet garni*, the lemon juice, and the peppercorns and salt. Cover the pot. Turn on a low flame, and cook only long enough to "sweat" the vegetables—that is, until moisture forms on their outsides (a few minutes).

Remove the cover and add the wine. Cook until reduced by half. Add the water, bring to a boil, then skim.

Simmer for about 20 minutes, then strain through cheesecloth or a fine *chinois*. Discard the solids and jar the fluid.

■ VEAL STOCK (N.Y.) ■

4 pounds veal bones
2 pounds veal meat,
   cubed
10 ounces carrots,
   peeled and cut into
   thick slices
8 ounces onions, peeled
   and cut into thick
   slices

5 ounces pork skin,
   blanched
2 cups boiling water
1 cup white wine
4 quarts water
bouquet garni (see
   Fish Stock)
a little salt

Put the bones and veal into a roasting pan and roast at 400°. Stir from time to time until well browned (but not black, Chef Daniel reminds us).

Put the vegetables into the bottom of a large cast-iron pot, then cover with the blanched pork skin (to blanch the skin, drop it into boiling water and allow to boil for a few minutes, then remove and discard the water). Pour the browned meat and bones over the skin, and allow to cook for about 20 minutes over a low flame.

Meanwhile, pour 2 cups of boiling water and 1 cup of white wine into the roasting pan to deglaze, dissolving everything left in the pan. Stirring to scrape the singed bits into the liquid, allow to boil in the roasting pan for a few minutes, then pour into the cast-iron pot.

Bring to the boil and reduce by half. Add the 4 quarts of water, the *bouquet garni*, and the salt.

Bring to the boil and let cook slowly, for about 6 hours, skimming often.

When done, allow to stand for about 30 minutes, then skim off all the fat. Pour through a *chinois* to get rid of the solids. The remaining liquid is your Veal Stock.

DUCK STOCK (N.Y.)

Yields about 2½ cups

duck bones and carcass
4 tablespoons sweet
butter
2 medium carrots,
diced small
2 medium onions,
diced small

4 stalks celery,
diced small
¼ cup Madeira
4 cups water
salt

Preheat your oven to 350°.

Brown the duck bones and carcass in the oven for about 45 minutes.

In a stockpot, melt the butter and brown the vegetables. Deglaze with a small amount of Madeira.

Add the bones, the water, and a little salt, and simmer, covered, for an hour.

Strain, and discard the solids.

GAME STOCK (N.Y.)

Yields about 2 quarts

This stock is used in Noisettes of Venison Grand Veneur (recipe on page 141), and the marinade called for is the Marinade in that recipe.

a few venison bones, split
3 medium carrots
3 small onions
2 quarts water
bouquet garni
½ cup chopped celery

3 peppercorns
bay leaf
teaspoon salt
2 tomatoes
3 cups Marinade (see
page 141)

In a roasting pan, brown the bones in a 375° oven.

Before they are golden brown, add the carrots and onions and continue to cook.

When the bones are brown, remove the pan from the oven, drain off any fat, and pour the bones and cooked vegetables into a soup pot.

Cover the bones with 2 quarts of water (or more, if needed, to cover), then add the remaining ingredients and simmer for 2-3 hours.

When cooked, strain off and discard everything but the stock.

Sauces

So often it is the flavor of the sauce that one remembers when thinking about a particularly tasty bit of French cuisine.

■ ▬▬▬▬▬SAUCE BÉCHAMEL (N.Y.)▬▬▬▬ ■

Yields about 2 cups

At the end of the cooking of this sauce, a 2-ounce piece of over-cooked veal will have to be removed before the sauce is put through a strainer. I snack on it myself, but my dogs always look as if they'd like to toss me for it.

3 tablespoons sweet butter	1 medium onion, chopped
3 tablespoons flour	2 ounces lean white veal
2 cups hot milk	few dashes nutmeg
salt	pinch of thyme
1 white peppercorn	

Over medium heat, melt the butter and stir in the flour. While the butter and flour cook for a few more minutes, continue to stir constantly. If you don't stir, the flour can make lumps. We cannot tolerate a bumpy Béchamel.

In another pan, bring your milk to the boil, and then add it to the butter and flour. Return the mixture to a boil and add salt and the peppercorn.

In a small frying pan, sear the onion and sear the veal on both sides, and then add to the first pan, along with the thyme and nutmeg.

Cook over a low flame for about 1 hour, then remove the veal and pass the rest through a fine strainer.

SAUCE HOLLANDAISE (N.Y.)

Yields about 1 cup

3 egg yolks, well beaten
2 tablespoons water
¾ cup (1½ sticks) melted
sweet butter,
cooled

½ lemon
salt, pepper, and
cayenne

Add the water to the egg yolks in the top of a double boiler, over a low flame (do not allow the water to come to a boil). Beat until thickened. Beat in the cooled melted butter and the juice squeezed from the ½ lemon. Season with salt, pepper, and cayenne—a dash of each, or to taste.

SAUCE BÉARNAISE (N.Y.)

Yields about 2 cups

Here is a sauce redolent of tarragon.
To crush the peppercorns, Chef Daniel suggests, place them on some parchment paper, then press them with the bottom of a heavy pot.

2 teaspoons finely
chopped shallots
2 ounces fresh
tarragon, chopped
1 ounce fresh
chervil, chopped
3 peppercorns, crushed
pinch salt
6 tablespoons vinegar

5 egg yolks
2 tablespoons water
¾ pound sweet butter,
melted
1 teaspoon chopped fresh
tarragon
1 teaspoon chopped fresh
chervil
dash cayenne pepper

Into a saucepan put the shallots, 2 ounces of chopped tarragon, an ounce of fresh chervil, 3 crushed peppercorns, a pinch of salt, and 6 tablespoons of vinegar. Cook over a medium flame to reduce by ⅔.

Remove from the fire and allow to cool a bit.

Whisk in the egg yolks and 2 tablespoons of water, until smooth.

Put the saucepan on top of a *bain-marie.*

Whisk in the butter a bit at a time, continuing to stir over the hot water until the sauce thickens.

Pass through a sieve, and finish with the addition of a teaspoon each of fresh chopped tarragon and chervil.

■ ■■■■■■■■MAYONNAISE (N.Y.)■■■■■■■ ■

Yields about 1½ cups

2 large egg yolks
1 teaspoon Dijon mustard
1 tablespoon wine
vinegar

1 teaspoon lemon juice
salt and white pepper
1 cup oil (½ olive,
½ corn)

In a mixing bowl, combine the egg yolks, mustard, vinegar, lemon juice, and salt and pepper. Whisk until the mixture is frothy.

Slowly, a bit at a time, drip in the oil, whisking in each dribble before adding more.

The mixture should be noticeably thicker by the time you get in half the oil. When most of the oil is in, taste to adjust the seasonings.

(Chef Dunas does not like to see this recipe turn out as thick as commercial mayonnaise. If it gets too thick, he recommends adding a few drops of boiling vinegar, or water, to thin it.)

Demiglace is an ingredient in several recipes. Usually, only a little of it at a time is needed. It seems silly to make a sauce with this many ingredients just to have 2 tablespoons. Let me suggest that you make it *before* it's needed, and refrigerate it. It will store for quite a while.

Demiglace itself is made up of three recipes: Brown Roux, Sauce Espagnole, and Veal Stock. Hang in.

BROWN ROUX:
¼ pound sweet butter
   (1 stick)
⅔ cup flour

SAUCE ESPAGNOLE:
¼ cup diced pork fat
1 carrot, diced
1 onion, diced
2 sprigs of fresh thyme
2 bay leaves
6 ounces Brown Roux

2 quarts Veal Stock
   (see page 157)
1 cup white wine
¾ cup thick tomato
   purée or tomato paste

DEMIGLACE:
Sauce Espagnole
Veal Stock (see
   page 157)

Madeira

To make the Brown Roux: Melt the butter in a heavy pan and simmer until it is clarified (perhaps as much as ½ an hour). Then add the flour and stir with a spatula. Heating slowly, cook for about 15 minutes, or until the mixture is a light golden color. This roux is to be used in the Sauce Espagnole. The Brown Roux can be made in advance and refrigerated.

Sauce Espagnole: Melt the diced pork fat in a heavy pot. Add the vegetables and herbs, and cook in the fat until lightly browned.

Drain off the fat and add the Brown Roux, the Veal Stock, the white wine, and the tomato purée.

Cook at low heat for 2 hours, skimming frequently.

The Demiglace itself: Now, to combine these into the Demiglace (a little fanfare, maestro, please).

The Demiglace itself is made by reducing some Sauce Espagnole (perhaps 1 cupful) by ⅔ (that's a lot of reduction), and then adding a little Veal Stock and a little Madeira wine to bring the Demiglace to the proper consistency.

To test the consistency, dip a wooden spoon into the sauce. Then hold the spoon sideways (so the bowl of the spoon is on edge), and wipe a finger sharply across the middle of the bowl of the spoon, through the sauce that's clinging to the spoon. That bare track created by your finger should stay; the sauce should not seep down to fill it. The sauce is now at the stage called *"nappé."*

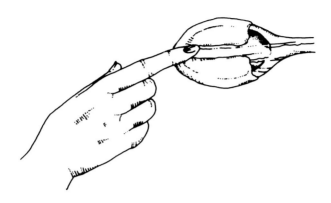

■■■■■■ VIN BLANC SAUCE (D.C.) ■■■■■ ■

Yields about 1½ cups

1⅓ cups Noilly Prat or other dry vermouth	1 tablespoon finely chopped shallots
1 cup Fish Stock (see page 156)	1 pint heavy cream
	salt and white pepper

Mix together the vermouth, stock, and shallots, and reduce until very thick.

In a second pan, reduce the cream by half.

Stir the two together thoroughly, and taste for the addition of salt and pepper.

■■■■■■ SAFFRON BUTTER (D.C.) ■■■■■ ■

Yields about 2 cups

Saffron is interesting stuff. It is the dried stigmata of a species of crocus. It not only colors the food yellow, but it has a distinctive spicy snap to it as well.

The last time I went shopping for saffron in the supermarket, I had to go to the discourtesy desk, where they took it from a locked case. Small wonder. At $4.59 for less than a gram, it came out to $183.60 an ounce: At this morning's setting, that's just over half the price of gold. (And gold doesn't cook well at all.) Saffron must be about the world's most expensive cooking substance.

2 teaspoons saffron	**1 pound sweet butter,**
1½ ounces dry white	**at room temperature**
wine	

In a small saucepan, combine the saffron and wine. Bring to a simmer, then shut off the flame and allow to stand for 10 minutes.

When the butter is at room temperature and quite soft, put it into a mixer with a paddle and turn it on (or mix with a wooden spoon by hand). Slowly add the saffron mixture and stir it in. Stop when the butter is smooth and the saffron is equally distributed throughout.

■■■■■■■■■■LAMB JUS (D.C.)■■■■■■■■■■

Yields about 1 quart

The herbs are called for in "bunches" because that is the way a restaurant buys them: tied into bunches. If you grow your own or buy them loose, about 4 tablespoons of each fresh herb should make a ¼ bunch.

10 pounds lamb bones	**¼ bunch each of thyme,**
(with very little fat)	**tarragon, rosemary**
3 medium onions, diced	**3 bay leaves**
small	**3 peppercorns**
½ bunch celery, diced	**1 cup tomato paste**
small	**2 cups white wine**
1 pound carrots, diced	
small	

Put the bones into a roasting pan and brown them in the oven at medium heat (about 350°).

When brown, remove from the oven. Take the bones out of the pan and reserve them, then pour off and discard most of the fat (Sous-Chef Tom Kelman recommends you get rid of 80% of the fat).

Add the vegetables and herbs and peppercorns, and brown in the remaining fat.

When the veggies are browned, stir in the tomato paste.

Add the white wine and stir until well mixed.

Place the bones and the vegetable mixture into a large kettle and add water until it is 6" above the other ingredients.

Simmer for 3-4 hours, then remove from the heat and strain. This is your Lamb Jus.

Lamb Fond: If you want Lamb Fond, reduce the Lamb Jus by ⅔, season with salt and pepper to taste, and strain through a *chinois*.

LOBSTER SAUCE (D.C.)
Sauce Américaine

Yields 1½ quarts

In the recipe for Lobster Bisque (see page 45) we described getting raw lobster bodies. They would work fine here. In this recipe, though, the shells or bodies are chopped or ground before being cooked.

½ cup olive oil	4 ounces cognac
4 lobster shells	4 ounces white wine
(ground-up or	1 quart Fish Stock
chopped)	(see page 156)
½ onion, diced	1 quart Chicken Stock
2 stalks celery, diced	(see page 155)
1 carrot, diced	⅔ cup Demiglace
⅓ cup tomato paste	(see page 162)
¾ cup chopped fresh	¼ lemon (cut in 2)
tarragon	¼ orange (cut in 2)
1 teaspoon fennel seeds	1/6 teaspoon cayenne
1 bay leaf	⅓ cup arrowroot starch
3 tablespoons thyme	salt
1 peppercorn	

Pour the olive oil into a large pot, and heat.

When hot, add the chopped-up lobster shells and cook until they get bright red.

Add the vegetables and cook until they are brown, then add the tomato paste and the herbs and the peppercorn. Stir in and heat.

Add half of the cognac (2 ounces), warm briefly, and *flambé*. Allow the flame to die a natural death.

Reduce the white wine by ⅔, and add it in, along with the stocks and Demiglace, and the citrus. Cook for 2 hours.

Skim off and discard the fat.

Add the cayenne, stir, then remove from the stove and strain through a *chinois*.

Place back on the stove and reduce by ⅓.

Dissolve the arrowroot starch in the remaining cognac, and stir in to thicken the sauce. Bring to the boil.

Taste for the possible addition of salt.

■■■■■■■FLAKY PASTRY (N.Y.)■■■■■■ ■

Welcome to the wonderful world of Flaky Pastry. This is grand stuff that can be used as a crust for other recipes (Steak and Kidney Pie or Pheasant Pâté), and has many other marvelous uses as well.

This is a pastry dough, not a bread dough; you don't need to knead it. Once it is mixed, the rolling pin does the work.

The butter should be somewhat softened. Not melted, and not soft —but taken out of the fridge and allowed to have the chill come off it.

A lot of cooks are afraid of pastry. Don't be: It's easy as pie.

1⅔ cups flour	**juice of ½ lemon**
(1 pound)	**cold water**
1½ teaspoons salt	**1 pound sweet butter**

Place the flour in a large bowl, and shape the center into a well.

Dissolve the salt in the lemon juice, and add a bit of water.

Mix the liquid into the flour gradually with your fingers, adding a bit more water at a time as needed. But be careful: The dough must not be soft. It should be about the same texture as the butter.

When you have enough water in, remove from the bowl, wrap in a clean cloth, and refrigerate for about 25 minutes.

Dust your pastry board (or, even better, your pastry marble) with flour. Unwrap the dough and put it on the board.

With your fingers, flatten and spread the dough into a disk shape, about 1″ thick.

Spread the butter over the dough, leaving about 2″ of the outside edge free of butter.

Lift a side edge, and fold it just over the middle. Lift the opposite edge and bring it all the way over (it should overlap, but not show excess).

Lift a top edge and fold it down, and then fold the bottom edge up.

All this folding should leave you with a square in front of you, with no butter showing.

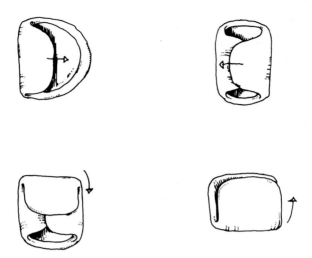

Wrap it in cloth again, and refrigerate for about 10 minutes. Don't keep it cold longer than that or the butter will harden, and you don't want that. While you will do lots more rolling, this is the last time you will form this square: It is only done to get the butter started into the pastry.

Now, you will begin the first of 6 rollings, referred to by Chef Daniel as the "*six tours*" — six turns.

Flour your board, and lay the pastry square on it. With a floured rolling pin, roll the pastry as long as you can on your board, making it about ½" thick.

Fold in 3 (bring one long end down, then the other end up and over).

Seal the 3 layers by pressing the edges with the rolling pin.

Turn the dough so that one set of edges faces you, and again roll out to about ½" thick, and again seal the edges with your rolling pin.

That ends the first "turn."

Rewrap the dough in the towel and refrigerate again for about 20 minutes.

It is all right to break up the *tours*, if it is more convenient that way: Do 4 *tours* today and 2 tomorrow, refrigerating the dough overnight. But allow some of the chill to come off before rolling out the dough at the beginning of the second day.

Dessert Table at th

∎ PART FOUR ∎

∎ SWEETS ∎

Desserts

Petits Fours

Frozen Raspberry Soufflé

English Sherry Trifle (here decorated with
chocolate syrup instead of red currant jelly)

▪ DESSERTS ▪

▪ ▬▬▬FROZEN RASPBERRY SOUFFLÉ (N.Y.)▬▬▬ ▪

Yields 10 soufflé cups and more than a cup of sauce

When I was a kid, I always ordered raspberry ice cream; when I went berry picking, I bypassed the thornless blueberries to battle the thorns for raspberries. You can imagine how I feel about this dish, which is the very soul of raspberries.

The recipe uses about 3 pints of raspberries in all: 1 pint for the sauce and 2 pints for the purée. The purée is simply mashed raspberries passed through a sieve to remove the seeds. Two pints of berries mash down to about 1 pint of purée.

The first time I made this frozen dessert at home, I used an extra pint of berries in the purée by mistake. We liked it so well, I've been doing it ever since.

At home, I do *not* strain the purée (I'm not worried about the seeds in my dentures), and I freeze everything in small, individual *baba-au-rhum* cups, rather than the individual soufflé cups used in the Jockey Club pastry kitchen.

1 quart heavy cream	**½ cup confectioners**
½ cup sugar	**sugar (for sauce)**
1 pint raspberry purée,	**extra whole berries**
strained	**(for garnish)**
3 whole eggs	**mint leaves (for**
3 egg yolks	**garnish)**
1 scant cup sugar	
1 pint raspberries (for	
sauce)	

Beat the cream, adding ½ cup of sugar a bit at a time, until it holds its peak.

Fold in the raspberry purée and then refrigerate the mixture.

In a *bain-marie* (or a large double boiler) on top of the stove, combine the eggs, the yolks, and the scant cup of sugar. Keep the flame very low or you will cook the eggs.

Whip the egg mixture until quite high and frothy, and a bit stiff (the eggs, not you).

Remove from the heat and continue to whip until the bowl feels somewhat cool.

Bring the whipped cream mixture out of the fridge and fold it into the eggs.

When all is well mixed, ladle it into small serving dishes and set into the freezer for at least 4 hours. At the New York Jockey Club, the pastry cook uses individual soufflé dishes with paper collars that extend an inch above the dish. Each collar is tied tightly in place with a piece of string around the soufflé dish. The batter is then poured in almost to the top of the collar.

While the soufflés are freezing, prepare the sauce.

Sauce: Take about a pint of raspberries, mash them (do not strain), and sprinkle ½ cup of confectioners sugar over the berries. Allow to stand at room temperature for a couple of hours, stirring occasionally.

Unmold the individual soufflés. Set on a serving dish, and spoon sauce over the top and around the base. Garnish the top with a whole raspberry surrounded by four mint leaves.

While these soufflés will keep quite a while in the freezer, Chef Daniel suggests, for best texture, that they be served within the first few days.

As a wine suggestion, try a Moulin-Touchais Anjou, 1964, from the Loire Valley.

Gâteau Grand Marnier, with a Marzipan topping

Marzipan can be used to "ice" any shape cake

■━━━━BURNT CREAM (N.Y.)■━━━━ ■
Crème Brûlée

Serves 6

1 quart heavy cream	**8 egg yolks**
1 vanilla bean	**powdered sugar (for**
1 tablespoon sugar	**dusting)**

Over a low flame, bring a quart of heavy cream with a vanilla bean in it to the boil.

Mix 1 tablespoon of sugar into 8 egg yolks.

Slowly, pour the hot cream over the yolks, stirring all the while. Pour the mixture back into the cream pan.

Cook over a very low flame, stirring continuously (taking care not to allow the mixture to boil) until it begins to thicken.

Remove the vanilla bean and pour the mixture into individual ramekins. Refrigerate overnight.

Next day, sprinkle the surfaces well with powdered sugar.

Brown by placing briefly in a salamander, or by putting under the broiler flame in your oven.

Set the ramekins on ice and serve.

■━━━━ENGLISH SHERRY TRIFLE (N.Y.)■━━━ ■

Yields a 2-quart trifle

Chef Daniel brought this recipe over from England, where it was very popular at the Connaught in London.

This Sponge Cake turns out so well that there are folks, we have heard, who don't use it in the trifle, but eat it plain. Of course, that may be just a rumor.

SPONGE CAKE:
4 large eggs
4 ounces sugar
½ teaspoon vanilla
  extract
1 scant cup flour

4 tablespoons sweet
  butter (melted and
  cooled)
additional butter and
  flour for pan

SAUCE ANGLAISE:
1 quart milk
6 egg yolks

½ cup sugar

TRIFLE:
1 Sponge Cake
blackberry jam
6 tablespoons sherry
2 tablespoons rum
Sauce Anglaise

whipped cream,
  sweetened with sugar
red currant jelly

Make the Sponge Cake: Preheat your oven to 350°.

Whisk the eggs and sugar over a *bain-marie* (or in the top of a large double boiler) until frothy (about 10 minutes). Be careful not to allow the water to get too hot; keep it just warm or the eggs will scramble.

Remove from the heat, add the vanilla extract, and beat until cool.

Fold in the flour.

Fold in the butter.

Rub the inside of a 6″ cake pan with a thin but complete layer of butter. Sprinkle some flour into the pan and shake until all the butter is floured, then tap out the excess flour.

Bake in a preheated 350° oven for about a ½ hour.

Make the Sauce Anglaise: Boil the milk.

Beat the egg yolks and sugar together until creamy.

Add the hot milk slowly, stirring all the while, so as not to cook the eggs. Return to the pan and thicken over a low flame, stirring, but do not allow to boil.

Assemble the Trifle: Slice the Sponge Cake in half horizontally, and spread both halves with blackberry jam. Cut into small cubes, and pile the cubes over the bottom of a 2-quart bowl.

Pour the sherry and rum over the cake, and leave to soak for 1 or 2 hours.

While it is still hot, pour the Sauce Anglaise over the soaked cake cubes, until all the cake is covered.

Refrigerate until well cooled.

Pile on a layer of whipped cream, then decorate the surface with a design made of the red currant jelly.

Coconut-Mousse Bombe, decorated with buttercream palm trees

Chocolate-Dipped Strawberries, Chocolate-Dipped Macademia Nuts, Tuilles

To make the design, cut a triangle out of parchment paper, about the size of half a sheet of writing paper, and fold into a little cone (this is a "cornet") with a closed tip. Fold the wide ends inside to keep it intact. Spoon in a teaspoon or so of red currant jelly, fold the top over, and cut off the barest end of the tip. Squeeze the cornet to make concentric circles on the surface of the whipped cream. A knife can then be drawn gently through the circles to create a spider-web design.

■ ■■■■■GRAND MARNIER MOUSSE (N.Y.)■■■■ ■

Yields about 4 quarts—enough for a large dinner party. The Jockey Club estimates that 4 quarts should serve 20

This lovely mousse is often served topped by berries in season.

In this recipe you are called on to cook a bit of sugar-water syrup to "soft-ball." A syrup has reached soft-ball when a few drops, spooned into some quite-cold water, can be fingered into a soft ball. If you have a candy thermometer, it should read about 275° F. (121° C.). Using a small amount of water, soft-ball will be quickly reached. If it gets beyond that, add some more water and try again. You really want it no harder than soft-ball.

1 quart heavy cream	10 egg yolks
⅓ cup sugar	⅓ cup dry white wine
1 cup sugar	1 cup Grand Marnier (or
¼ cup water	more, to taste)

Whip the cream in a large bowl (start slowly or you'll spatter it over the kitchen), adding ⅓ cup of sugar, a tablespoon or 2 at a time. Whip to hard-peak, then refrigerate.

Put 1 cup of sugar and ¼ cup of water into a saucepan, over medium heat. Cook until it reaches the "soft-ball" stage.

Clean all "grease" from the cream off your beaters, and beat the yolks in a *bain-marie* over very low heat; too high a flame will cook egg around the sides of the bowl.

When the yolks are creamy, remove from the heat, and continue to beat. After a few minutes, beat in the white wine. When the wine is well beaten in, continue the beating and drip in the sugar syrup.

Continue to beat, and when eggs are fairly stiff, add Grand Marnier, tasting after 1 cup is added. Do keep in mind when you taste that the whipped cream will still have to be worked in, and that dilutes the flavor.

When stiff, and somewhat cool, fold in the whipped cream well, using a large-bladed spatula.

Pour into two 2-quart bowls, and refrigerate for an hour or so.

If you would like a wine with this dessert, try, from the Rhône, a Muscat de Beaum de Venise, by Prosper Maufoux.

■ ■■■■■■CHOCOLATE MOUSSE (N.Y.)■■■■■ ■

Yields about 4 quarts

We buy chocolate in 10-pound blocks from a local candy maker— it is rich, and of excellent flavor and quality. You may have to search for an appropriate chocolate. We found the supermarket stuff convenient, but of second-rate flavor. When I first tasted this at the New York Jockey Club (I didn't really "taste" it: I took home a 2-quart bowlful), it was made with imported Swiss chocolate.

If you've never made one, a Chocolate Mousse is not just a pale chocolate pudding. The texture is firm (it will hold your dessert spoon upright) but light, and above all creamy. Every mouthful should shout "CHOCOLATE!" at you.

1 quart heavy cream	1 cup sugar
¼ cup sugar	1 cup water
12 ounces semisweet chocolate	10 egg yolks
	2 ounces dry white wine

Starting at slow speed (so as not to spatter), begin to whip the cream. As it begins to rise, increase the speed and add the ¼ cup sugar, a bit at a time. Beat to the stiff-peak stage. Reserve in the refrigerator.

Chop the chocolate into small bits and put into the top of a double boiler to melt over low heat. (Chocolate should always be melted over low heat.)

Combine the cup of sugar and the water in a saucepan, and cook over medium heat until it reaches the soft-ball stage.

Meanwhile, wash your beaters thoroughly (to get rid of the oil from the cream) and put your egg yolks into the top of a *bain-marie*, over low heat. Beat the eggs until warm and quite creamy.

When the yolks are creamy, remove from the heat, and continue to beat until quite risen—perhaps as much as 10 minutes.

Beat in the white wine, until thick again.

Continuing to beat, slowly drip in the sugar syrup. There is no need to allow the syrup to cool, so long as you drip it in slowly.

When the eggs are fairly thick, beat in the chocolate, until thoroughly mixed.

Now, fold in the whipped cream, until smooth and uniform in color.

Pour into two 2-quart bowls and refrigerate for at least 2 hours before serving.

■——————CONCORD CAKE (N.Y.)——————■

Yields 2 large cakes

This is a chocolate lover's dream. It is a cake with no flour at all. It is composed of two meringues: a hard-baked biscuit meringue and a buttery chocolate meringue.

The Biscuit Meringue recipe makes enough for two cakes; the Crème recipe makes enough for one cake, but it is easily doubled. The Biscuit Meringue will keep indefinitely in any dry place, but the Crème is less durable. Make the full Biscuit Meringue recipe, then store the extra until you are ready for a second Concord Cake. The Biscuit Meringue makes a lovely snack by itself.

You'll need baker's parchment for the Biscuit Meringue: This is a treated paper product that eliminates the need for greasing. Without the parchment, you'd have to grease all your baking trays—and even then you'd have trouble getting the biscuit rounds off intact. I found parchment in my local supermarket.

For both recipes you will need a large pastry bag, with a medium-large and a large nozzle (plain).

BISCUIT MERINGUE:
2 cups egg whites
2 generous cups sugar
3 cups confectioners
   sugar

1¾ cups cocoa powder

CRÈME:
14 ounces semisweet
   chocolate
¾ cup egg whites
¼ cup sugar

1¾ sticks sweet
   butter (at room
   temperature)

Make the Biscuit Meringue: Beat together 2 cups of egg whites and 2 cups of sugar until moderately stiff.

Sift the confectioners sugar and cocoa together and then gently fold them into this meringue.

Shape the Biscuit: Take 4 large baking sheets and cover them with baker's parchment.

Put a ¼" plain nozzle on your pastry bag and half fill the bag with meringue.

You are going to squeeze out 4 flat disks, about ⅜" thick and 9" across—2 per sheet on 2 sheets, without touching.

Start at the center of the disk and squeeze the meringue out in a closed spiral—you don't want any open spaces, but you don't want the meringue too thick or you won't have enough. Remember, 2 per sheet, not touching. If you leave an open space in the spiral, go over it with an extra squeeze: These Biscuit Meringue disks will not be seen in the finsihed cake—they are covered by the Crème.

When the disks are finished, put those sheets aside, and, on the 2 empty sheets, squeeze out long thin rods of meringue. Again, don't let them touch. These rods will later be cut up and crushed to be the outer covering of the cake.

Bake the Biscuit: Bake in a 225° oven until all the meringue is cooked hard. (About 2½ hours—or more.) You can test by breaking into one of the tubes: It will be darker inside, but there should be no wetness.

When baked, put the Biscuit Meringue aside to cool, and make the Crème.

Making the Crème: Break up (or cut up) the chocolate and put it into the top of a double boiler over moderate heat to melt.

Make the meringue by beating ¾ cup egg whites, and adding ¼ cup sugar slowly, as the whites work up. Reserve.

Put the softened butter into a mixing bowl and beat it briefly.

Add the melted chocolate to the butter and beat until creamy and cooled (a minute or so). Start all your beating at low speed: Chocolate spatters.

Fold the meringue gently into the chocolate mixture.

Assembling the Cake: Place one Biscuit Meringue disk onto a 9" cake cardboard.

Put your large plain nozzle into your pastry bag, and half fill the bag with the Crème.

Starting at the center of the disk, squeeze out a thick layer in a closed touching spiral, almost out to the edge. Stop, then come back to the center and repeat, making a second layer of Crème right on top of the first.

Your total layer of "filling" should be about 1½" high—but you have leeway, so long as you have enough Crème left to coat the outside of the cake.

Place a second Biscuit Meringue on top of the Crème and put the unfinished cake into the refrigerator or freezer for a while to help it harden a bit.

Meanwhile, cut up the biscuit rods into 1" (or less) bits. The rods will crumble as you cut. That's fine.

Remove the cake from the cold and "ice" it with the rest of the Crème, filling in the sides and slathering a layer on top. This is most easily done by holding the cake in one hand and working with a spatula in the other. There should be no biscuit showing.

When all the Crème is on, hold the cake over a baking sheet (so you can reclaim whatever falls) and press on the cut-up bits of rod by the handful. Every bit of Crème should be covered with this cut-up and crumbled biscuit. (Remember, you are using only *half* your cut-up rods for this cake; you have 2 more disks, and will make another cake soon.)

When finished, refrigerate or freeze. I freeze the cake, and it keeps marvelously well (and cuts marvelously well, frozen). But it also can be served same-day, just chilled in the refrigerator. The butter and chocolate firm up very nicely.

■■■■WHITE CHOCOLATE MOUSSE (D.C.)■■■ ■

Yields about 2 quarts

This is for those of you who like your desserts *sweet*. White chocolate tastes different from brown—it is sweeter and smoother and, of course, has no cocoa bitterness. And it must be heated more carefully. Pastry Chef Danny Michel suggests using a *bain-marie* or double boiler, with the water just heated but not boiling. Heat the chocolate long enough to melt it thoroughly, but not so long or so hot as to make it grainy.

To our taste, this recipe is all the better for the loss of a couple of tablespoons of sugar. *De gustibus* . . .

12 ounces white chocolate	**1 cup egg whites**
chocolate	**½ cup sugar**
1 pint heavy cream	

Melt the chocolate, and allow it to cool a little.

Whip the cream to soft-peak and reserve in the refrigerator.

Whip the egg whites to soft-peak, adding the sugar as they increase.

Fold the chocolate into the egg whites, then fold in the whipped cream.

Refrigerate until cold.

■ ■■■■■■HAZELNUT MOUSSE (D.C.)■■■■■ ■

Yields almost 4 quarts, or enough for 20 six-ounce servings

This is a unique mousse, with crunchy bits of hazelnut to pique the palate. It is quite rich, and just as usable as a cake filling or even an icing (when chilled).

The "hazelnut paste" and "hazelnut grasse" called for in the recipe are commercial products, hard to find for the home kitchen, but they are relatively simple to imitate. The paste is finely ground-up roasted hazelnuts (hazelnut butter). If your blender or processor will make peanut butter, it should have no trouble making hazelnut butter (or paste). About 1 cup of nuts should make about ½ cup of paste.

Hazelnut grasse is sweetened hazelnut paste. Instead, I used about ⅓ cup paste with 2 tablespoons of honey, combined in the blender. Also, I confess it, I used unroasted nuts.

10 egg yolks	⅓ cup hazelnut grasse
1 cup sugar	1 cup roasted hazelnuts,
4 ounces Frangelica	chopped fine
liqueur	1 quart heavy cream
⅓ ounce gelatin	whipped cream flavored
½ cup strong coffee	with Frangelica and
(cold)	Kahlua (for garnish)
¼ pound butter (room	whole roasted hazelnuts
temperature)	(for garnish)
½ cup unsweetened	
hazelnut paste	

Combine the yolks, sugar, and 4 ounces of Frangelica, and whip over hot (not boiling) water until quite thick and pale (about 10 minutes), and then remove from the heat and whip until cool (about 5 more minutes).

Combine the gelatin and coffee and allow to swell for about 10 minutes. Then heat the mixture until just melted, and allow it to return to room temperature. Don't keep it hanging around too long or it will solidify.

Combine the soft butter, paste, grasse, and chopped nuts, mixing well.

Whip the cream to soft-peak.

Fold the hazelnut-and-butter mix into the yolks.

Fold in the gelatin.

Fold in the cream, and refrigerate.

Dot the center of each serving with a dollop of whipped cream flavored with Frangelica and Kahlua liqueurs and a whole hazelnut.

■■■■■■■■RICE PUDDING (D.C.)■■■■■■■■

Yields 12 custard cups

When I was a kid, my idea of a treat was to visit the Automat for a serving of rice pudding. Aside from the rice, there is scant resemblance between that rice pudding and this.

1 cup white rice	4 egg yolks
6 cups light cream	½ cup raisins
½ a vanilla bean,	½ cup Myers Rum
split	water
1 cup sugar	1 quart heavy cream

Cook the rice slowly in the light cream, with the vanilla bean, until the rice is quite soft and appears overcooked.

Mix together the sugar and egg yolks.

When mixed, add a tablespoon of the cooked rice to the egg mixture to temper it. Then, stirring constantly, slowly add the yolk mixture to the rice. (This has the effect of cooking the yolks somewhat.)

Allow this mixture to come to room temperature.

Plump the raisins: Put them in a saucepan with the rum, then add enough water to cover. Simmer for about 10 minutes, then allow to cool.

Whip 1 quart of heavy cream to soft-peak.

Fold the whipped cream into the rice. The rice mixture must be soft enough to accept the whipped cream without deflating it completely. If the rice mixture is too dense, soften it with the addition of a little milk or light cream.

Divide the plumped raisins among 12 small ovenproof custard cups, then spoon in the pudding.

Glaze golden brown by placing quite briefly under a broiler or salamander.

Refrigerate and serve cold.

JOCKEY CLUB HARLEQUIN CHEESECAKE (D.C.)

Yields 1 very rich 10" cake

I have been assured (threatened is closer to the truth) by Pastry Chef Danny Michel that the most important thing with cheesecake is to get a *smooth batter* with *no lumps*.

3 ounces semisweet chocolate

3 pounds cream cheese, at room temperature

1 cup sour cream, at room temperature

2 cups sugar

½ teaspoon vanilla extract

½ teaspoon orange extract

4 eggs

orange juice (to thin, if necessary)

CRUST:

14 ounces finely ground graham-cracker crumbs

9 ounces melted sweet butter

butter for greasing

Preheat your oven to 300°.

Melt the chocolate in a large bowl, over hot water, and remove from the heat. Reserve.

Mix the cream cheese and sour cream together, scraping and remixing several times until *smooth*.

Add the sugar and the two extracts, and blend in.

Whisk the eggs only a few times and add them to the cheese. Mix and scrape a few more times.

If the batter is a pourable texture, go on to the next step; if not, mix in a little orange juice until it is pourable.

Pour about ⅓ of the batter into the chocolate, and mix well. Reserve the remaining batter.

Thin the chocolate batter to pouring consistency (if needed) with an ounce or so of orange juice.

Make the Crust: Combine the crumbs and butter, mixing very well.

Coat the inside of a 10" ring mold with a generous layer of butter.

Press the crust mixture against the insides of the mold, starting at the sides of the mold and then coating the bottom.

Assemble and Bake: Now, layer the batters: Pour about half of the plain batter into the mold, then a layer consisting of all the chocolate, then the rest of the plain, filling the mold with all your batter.

Bake at 300°-325° until ¾ set, about 1½ hours. The center will still shake like Jello and there will be no browning. Remove the cake from the oven, allow to cool. Refrigerate overnight, and the cake will be ready to serve.

■■■■STRAWBERRIES ROMANOFF (D.C.)■■■■

Yields 2 generous servings

Here is a dish prepared near your table by a Jockey Club captain. When you prepare it at home, flourishes are optional.

**20 large ripe
  strawberries
1 ounce Cointreau
1 ounce Grand Marnier
splash Courvoisier
2 small scoops vanilla
  ice cream**

**2 small scoops whipped
  cream
additional whipped
  cream (for decoration)
2 strawberries (for
  decoration)**

In a large bowl, mash the 20 berries into a paste with the back of a spoon.

Add the alcohols, 2 scoops of ice cream, the whipped cream, then fork-blend it all together and scrape into 2 serving bowls. (This delicious dish should have about the consistency of yoghurt.)

Decorate each bowl with a dab of whipped cream at the four quadrants and another dab in the center, with a strawberry atop the center dab.

■■■■COCONUT-MOUSSE BOMBE (D.C.)■■■ ■

Yields 2 bombes

This spectacular dessert is made of three separate elements: Coconut Mousse, Chocolate Sponge Cake, and a soft chocolate covering called a Ganache. They are all combined in this dome-shaped delicacy called a "bombe."

The recipe is complex and takes a lot of work, but follow it step by step and applause awaits.

Each of the bombes should give you a dozen slices—so the two bombes are plenty for a good-sized dinner party.

CHOCOLATE SPONGE CAKE:
- 1⅓ cups cake flour
- 1 cup cornstarch
- 1⅓ cups cocoa powder
- "a good-sized pinch" baking soda (about 1/16 teaspoon)
- 15 eggs
- 2 cups sugar
- 3 tablespoons melted sweet butter
- butter and flour (for cake pans)

PASTRY CREAM:
- 2 cups milk
- ½ cup sugar
- ⅓ cup cornstarch
- 2 whole eggs
- 2 egg yolks
- 4 tablespoons sweet butter

COCONUT MOUSSE:
- ⅞ cup coconut cream (½ can Coco Lopez)
- 1 pint toasted coconut
- 3½ cups Pastry Cream
- 1 ounce gelatin (4 packets)
- 1 cup cold water
- 1 quart heavy cream
- 1 ounce coconut liqueur
- 1 cup egg whites
- ½ cup sugar

GANACHE:
- 1¼ pounds semisweet chocolate
- 2 cups heavy cream
- toasted coconut (optional)

Chocolate Sponge Cake: Preheat your oven to about 350°.

Combine the flour, cornstarch, cocoa powder, and baking soda, and sift twice, or until they are well mixed.

Combine the eggs and sugar in a *bain-marie* (or the top of a large double boiler), and stir until barely warmed.

Remove from the heat and whip at high speed until the mixture has completely risen and begins to recede slightly (you will see a "high-water" ring in the bowl).

Fold in the flour mixture.

Fold in the melted and cooled (but still liquid) butter.

Bake in three 8″ cake pans, buttered and floured, for about 25-30 minutes (at 350° F.). The cake is done when the center springs back when pressed lightly. Turn out immediately, cool at room temperature, then wrap in plastic and refrigerate until cold. (Sponge cake slices better when chilled.)

Pastry Cream: Combine 2 cups of milk and ¼ cup of sugar in a saucepan and bring to a boil.

Separately, combine the remaining ¼ cup of sugar and the ⅓ cup cornstarch.

Mix 1 egg into the starch-sugar mixture until you get a smooth paste, then mix in the remaining egg and the 2 yolks.

Temper the eggs with a few tablespoons of the hot milk, then pour the egg mix into the milk slowly, stirring all the while.

Stir until the mixture thickens; allow it to come to a boil, then stir again; then remove. We want it to thicken, not scorch.

Off the heat, stir in the butter.

Allow to cool to room temperature.

Coconut Mousse: Add the coconut cream and toasted coconut to the room-temperature Pastry Cream. (If the Pastry Cream was made earlier and refrigerated, set it in a *bain-marie* until it comes to room temperature.)

Combine 1 ounce of gelatin and 1 cup of water and allow to swell (or "bloom") for 10 minutes, then warm briefly until it dissolves.

Whip a quart of heavy cream with an ounce of coconut liqueur to soft-peak, and reserve.

Whip 1 cup of egg whites and ½ cup of sugar until soft-peak.

Mix the gelatin with the Pastry Cream.

Fold in the whipped egg whites.

Fold in the whipped cream, and set aside for a moment.

Take the Sponge Cakes out of the refrigerator and carefully cut into layers ⅜″ thick. You will need 6 layers for the 2 bombes.

Assembling the Bombes: Take two 8½″ bombe molds (or two deep mixing bowls of the same width) and line the insides with plastic wrap.

You are going to put alternating layers of cake and mousse into the mold.

The first layer is cake; cut a disk of sponge about 4" across, and put it in the bottom of the mold. (When you turn the mold over to get the bombe out, this 4" circle will be on top.)

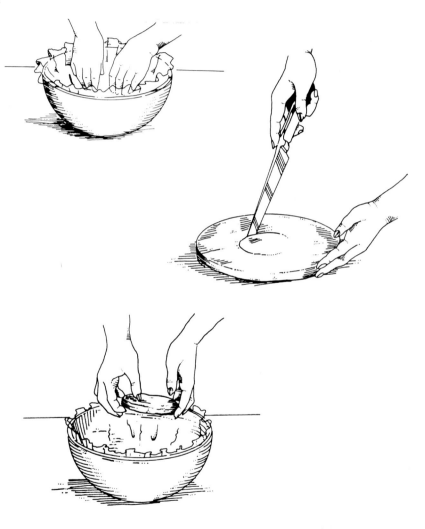

For the second layer, pour in a couple of inches of mousse.

Cut the next layer of sponge to fit (mine was a 7" disk), and place it on top of the mousse.

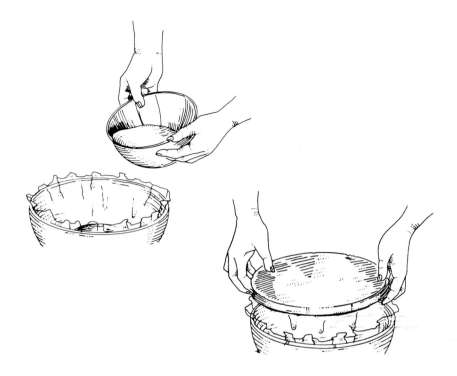

Pour in more mousse, to within a ½" of the top.

Place a final slice of sponge over the mousse (one whole 8" layer) —and you have filled one mold. Repeat for the second bombe.

Refrigerate until quite cold.

Ganache: Chop the chocolate into small bits and put it in a mixing bowl.

Bring the cream to a boil, then pour it over the chocolate, and stir well until smooth. Don't beat.

(Ganache will not harden as will ordinary melted chocolate, and it will not stay sticky, as will chocolate sauce.)

Remove the bombes from the refrigerator.

Cut a cake cardboard to just fit the bottom of each bombe.

Put the cardboards on top, then turn the molds over; the bombes should come out easily. If they don't turn out immediately, dip briefly in warm water. When out, remove the plastic wrap.

Place the bombes on a wire rack over baking trays (or anything to catch the Ganache as it drips off).

Pour the Ganache over the bombe, covering the entire surface. The excess will drip through the wire rack.

When all dripped out, lift the bombe off the wire rack. (After the second bombe is covered, the excess Ganache can be scraped up and stored in the refrigerator.)

You can finish off the bottoms with a little toasted coconut pressed over the bottom inch. (Pastry Chef Danny Michel ornaments this recipe with a mocha buttercream drawing of some coconut palm trees.)

Refrigerate an hour or so, until the Ganache is not sticky.

With or without the palm tree drawings, these Bombes are a blast.

Ice Creams and Sorbets (N.Y.)

If you have an ice-cream machine, crank it up, because these recipes from the New York Jockey Club give you desserts more delicious than anything from a cardboard box.

■■■■■■VANILLA ICE CREAM■■■■■■

Yields about 3 quarts

MIXTURE #1:
3 cups milk   1 cup sugar
1 quart heavy cream   1 vanilla bean

MIXTURE #2:
20 egg yolks (about   1½ cups milk
   1½ cups)   1 cup sugar

Combine Mixture #1 in a 6-quart pot, and bring to the boil over a slow flame. The longer the mixture takes to get to the boil, the more vanilla flavor is extracted from the bean.

Combine 20 egg yolks with 1½ cups of milk and 1 cup of sugar to make Mixture #2.

Temper Mixture #2 with a few tablespoons of #1, stirred in well; and then slowly add #2 to #1, over a low flame, stirring all the while. Do not allow it to come to a boil.

When the two mixtures are combined, remove from the heat and allow to cool. (We set the mixture in the refrigerator until it gets to room temperature. Starting with a hot mix can double the freezing time in the ice-cream maker.)

When at room temperature, freeze according to your ice-cream machine's instructions.

CHOCOLATE ICE CREAM

Yields more than 3 quarts

This is just Vanilla Ice Cream with the addition of chocolate.

**12 ounces semisweet
chocolate**

a small pinch of salt

**MIXTURE #1:
same as #1 of Vanilla
Ice Cream**

**MIXTURE #2:
same as #2 of Vanilla
Ice Cream**

Melt the chocolate in a *bain-marie* or double boiler.

Make Mixture #1, in a large (6-quart) pot, and when hot, add the melted chocolate. Bring to a boil over a low flame.

Proceed as above with Vanilla Ice Cream (tempering, combining, cooling, and making the ice cream).

STRAWBERRY ICE CREAM

Yields about 1½ quarts.

The next time you make Vanilla Ice Cream (recipe on page 196), set aside a cup of the final mixture, or of the made ice cream, for this delicious concoction.

**1½ cups sugar
⅔ cup water
1 pint strawberries,
mashed**

**juice of ½ lemon
1 cup Vanilla Ice Cream
mix**

Combine the sugar and water in a pan and bring to the boil.

Stir in the strawberries and lemon juice.

Add the unfrozen Vanilla Ice Cream, stir well, and freeze.

SORBETS

A sorbet is a French sherbet. Ours here are made without milk or cream.

■■■■■■■■■■■■■MELON SORBET■■■■■■■■■■■■

Yields a bit more than 1 quart

Cantaloupe is the preferred melon for this sorbet. I get my juice by using fresh melon and a juicer. This sorbet is only as tasty as the melons you use—the sweeter the better.

1 quart melon juice　　　　　　**juice of ½ lemon**
3 tablespoons sugar

Combine all the ingredients and freeze in an ice-cream maker.

■■■■■■■■■■■■■LEMON SORBET■■■■■■■■■■■■

Yields about ½ gallon

1 quart cold water　　　　　　**1 pint lemon juice,**
2 cups sugar　　　　　　　　　　**pits strained out**
⅓ ounce lemon zest

Combine the water, sugar, and lemon zest in a pot and bring to the boil, then allow to cool.

When cool, add the lemon juice, strain out the bits of zest, and freeze in an ice-cream maker.

■■■■■■■■■■■STRAWBERRY SORBET■■■■■■■■■■

Yields about ½ gallon

As with Melon Sorbet, above, the juice can be made in a juicer. You will need about 2 quarts of berries to make 1 quart of juice.

1 pint water　　　　　　　　**1 quart strawberry juice**
2 cups sugar

Combine the water and sugar in a pot and bring to the boil, then allow to cool.

Strain the seeds from the juice (if there are any—my juicer strains automatically), add the juice to the sugar-water syrup, and freeze in an ice-cream maker.

■━━━━━RASPBERRY SORBET ━━━━■

Yields about 1½ quarts

¾ cup water	**1 quart raspberry juice,**
1¾ cups sugar	**seeds strained**

Combine the water and sugar in a pot and bring to the boil. When cooled, stir in the strained juice and freeze in an ice-cream machine.

■━━━━━QUATRE FLEURS ━━━━■

Yields about 1½ quarts

The four "flowers" ("*fleurs*") are the four fruit flavors in this sorbet. The fruits must be ripe and sweet.

1½ tablespoons water	**juice of ½ a ripe**
1½ tablespoons sugar	**pineapple**
1 pint fresh orange	**scant 1½ cups fork-**
juice	**mashed banana pulp**
1 cup fresh lemon juice	

In a small pan, heat the water and dissolve the sugar. When cooled, combine all the ingredients and freeze in an ice-cream maker.

■■■■GÂTEAU MARJOLAINE (D.C.)■■■■ ■

Yields 1 large gâteau

Here is a cake with 7 layers and several parts, but not difficult to put together. The cake portion is a form of "Japonnaise"; the fillings are Chocolate Whipped Cream, Praline Filling, and Grand Marnier Whipped Cream; the covering is Ganache.

The praline paste called for in the Praline Filling is a commercial product. If you can't find it, you have the Jockey Club kitchen's authorization to substitute the sweetened hazelnut paste we made in Hazelnut Mousse, page 187.

Plan to keep the cake refrigerated overnight—it improves with holding for a day or so.

JAPONNAISE:

7 ounces almond flour (or finely ground almonds)	**1¼ cups sugar (divided in half)**
5 ounces roasted hazelnuts, finely ground	**8 egg whites (large) butter (for greasing) flour (for flouring)**
3 tablespoons flour	

CHOCOLATE WHIPPED CREAM:

6 ounces semisweet chocolate	**1 cup heavy cream**

PRALINE FILLING:

4 tablespoons praline paste	**1 cup heavy cream**
4 tablespoons sweet butter	

GRAND MARNIER WHIPPED CREAM:

6 tablespoons butter	**1 tablespoon powdered sugar**
1¼ cups heavy cream	
1 ounce Grand Marnier	

GANACHE:

1 pound semisweet chocolate	**1½ cups heavy cream**

Japonnaise: Preheat your oven to 425°.

Combine the almond flour (finely ground almonds will do), ground hazelnuts, flour, and about half the sugar (about ¾ cup), and mix well.

Beat the egg whites, gradually adding the remaining sugar (about ½ cup), to soft-peak, and fold into the dry ingredients.

To make the Japonnaise you will need a large baking sheet (about 14″ by 24″) to form one large layer.

Lightly butter and flour a sheet of baker's parchment, at least 14″ by 24″, and place it in the tray (butter side up, of course).

Scrape the Japonnaise mix onto the sheet and spread out to a layer 14″ by 24″ and about ¼″ to ⅜″ thick, keeping the edges as straight as you can.

Bake at 425° for 10 to 15 minutes, or until a bit dry and slightly browned. *Be careful not to scorch it.*

Remove from the oven, and immediately cut into 4 strips, 3½″ by 24″. Allow the cut strips to cool.

Chocolate Whipped Cream: Melt 6 ounces of chocolate in the top of a double boiler or in a *bain-marie*, and allow it to cool until just warm against your lip.

Whip 1 cup of heavy cream until a bit softer than soft-peak.

The combining of the chocolate and cream is typical of the combining in this recipe, and should be followed closely: Pour all the chocolate into the cream and whisk vigorously for a few seconds, then stop. More beating will make butter. If the chocolate is not evenly distributed, fold in gently with a few turns of a spatula.

(Note: All of these cream fillings should be used as soon as they are made.)

Praline Filling: Combine commercial praline paste (or the sweetened hazelnut paste we used in Hazelnut Mousse, page 187) with 4 tablespoons of butter, warming and stirring in a saucepan until smooth.

Whip a cup of heavy cream until soft-peak, then combine as we did with the Chocolate Whipped Cream: Pour all the warm mixture into the cream, then a few seconds of vigorous whipping, then stop.

Grand Marnier Whipped Cream: Melt 6 tablespoons of butter and allow to cool until just warm; whip 1¼ cups of heavy cream and an ounce of Grand Marnier and the powdered sugar to soft-peak; fold in the butter.

Assembling the Gâteau: Carefully remove one of the strips of Japonnaise from the parchment and place it on a baking sheet. Spread a layer of the Chocolate Whipped Cream over it, about ½″ thick.

Place another rectangle of Japonnaise on top, and refrigerate for about 15 minutes (to solidify the filling).

Remove from the fridge and lay down a similar layer of the Praline Filling; cover with a strip of Japonnaise, and again refrigerate for 15 minutes.

Remove from the fridge again, and top with a layer of the Grand Marnier Whipped Cream, and cover with the last layer of Japonnaise. Wrap well with plastic wrap, and store in the refrigerator overnight. (Perhaps a refrigerator with a revolving door would help.)

Ganache (Next Day): Chop a pound of chocolate into fine bits; bring 1½ cups of cream just to the boil, then pour over the chocolate and mix easily (don't introduce air).

Cover and allow to cool and thicken at room temperature to the consistency of buttercream, then spread over the cake with a spatula.

Allow the cake to stand at least 24 hours, refrigerated, before serving. The Japonnaise absorbs some of the fluid from the fillings and softens (which is desirable) as it stands.

Cut into ¾″ slices to serve; should yield 32 slices (if my arithmetic is correct).

Soufflés (D.C.)

For many, soufflés lie at the heart of French dessert cooking.

These recipes can be made in any size soufflé dish, though in Washington they are prepared in individual dishes.

The dishes should be buttered, and then sugared before the soufflé mixture is poured in (spread butter by fingers over the insides and rim, and then pour in sugar — turn the dish to allow the sugar to get into all corners, and then pour out the excess sugar into the next individual soufflé dish).

As a final hint from Pastry Chef Danny Michel, the bowl, the whip, and all the ingredients should be at room temperature.

All these recipes depend on Pastry Cream, which should be made in advance and can be kept refrigerated. Rice flour can be found in Oriental food stores, or sometimes in health-food stores.

■■■■■■■■■PASTRY CREAM■■■■■■■■■

2 quarts milk	**1 cup sugar (additional)**
2 cups sugar	**16 egg yolks**
1 pound rice flour	

Combine the milk and 2 cups of sugar in a large pan and place over medium heat until just *before* it comes to the boil.

Sift well together the rice flour and 1 cup of sugar.

Add half the yolks and beat to a smooth paste. Mix in the remaining yolks.

Temper the egg mixture with a little of the hot milk mixture. Then slowly add the egg mixture to the milk, over a low flame, stirring constantly, and allow to just come to the first boil or two, to assure that all the starch is cooked.

■■■■■■■■■■RASPBERRY SOUFFLÉ■■■■■■■■ ■

Yields 1 individual soufflé

You may have met raspberry reduction before: overripe raspberries very slowly cooked down to a sixth. That is, 6 cups of raspberries yields 1 cup of reduction.

Framboise is a raspberry brandy.

⅛ cup (minus 1 teaspoon) raspberry reduction
⅛ cup (plus 1 teaspoon) Pastry Cream (recipe above)

Framboise (optional)
2 egg whites (at room temperature)
2 tablespoons sugar

Preheat your oven to 400 °.

Mix the raspberry reduction and the Pastry Cream together, to form the soufflé base. If it is too thick to fold in easily, thin out with a bit of Framboise.

Beat the egg whites, and, as they begin to form, add the sugar a bit at a time and whip to a soft-peak meringue.

Fold the soufflé base into the meringue, then pour into a buttered and sugared soufflé dish. The mixture should just fill the dish.

Put into a 400° oven and bake for about 8-10 minutes.

■━━━━━━LEMON SOUFFLÉ━━━━━━■

Yields 1 soufflé

LEMON SYRUP:

2 tablespoons lemon juice	**about ¼ teaspoon lemon zest**
2 tablespoons sugar	

SOUFFLÉ

⅛ cup Lemon Syrup	**2 egg whites (at room temperature)**
⅛ cup Pastry Cream (see page 202)	**2 tablespoons sugar**

To make the Lemon Syrup, cook the lemon juice, sugar, and zest in a small saucepan briefly, until thick.

Preheat your oven to 400°.

Combine the Lemon Syrup and the Pastry Cream to make the soufflé base.

Beat the egg whites. As they begin to foam, add 2 tablespoons of sugar a bit at a time, to make a soft-peak meringue.

Fold the soufflé base into the meringue, then scrape into an individual soufflé dish that has been buttered and sugared as described above.

Bake at 400° for 8-10 minutes.

■━━━━━━CHOCOLATE SOUFFLÉ━━━━━━■

Yields 2 individual soufflés

This is the favorite at the D.C. Jockey Club.

CHOCOLATE FLAVOR:

2 tablespoons sugar	**cocoa powder, sifted**
3 tablespoons hot tap water	

SOUFFLÉ:

¼ cup chocolate flavor	**4 egg whites (at room temperature)**
¼ cup Pastry Cream (recipe on page 202)	**5 tablespoons sugar**

To make the Chocolate Flavor, mix together 2 tablespoons of sugar and 3 tablespoons of hot tap water, and stir until dissolved; then add enough sifted cocoa powder to make a smooth paste.

Preheat your oven to 400°.

Mix together the Chocolate Flavor and the Pastry Cream to make the soufflé base.

Beat the egg whites, and, as they thicken, add the sugar a bit at a time to make a soft-peak meringue.

Fold the soufflé base into the meringue, and scrape into 2 buttered and sugared individual soufflé dishes, as described above.

Bake at 400° for 8-10 minutes.

■■■■■■GRAND MARNIER SOUFFLÉ■■■■■ ■

Yields 1 individual soufflé

It almost always takes more Grand Marnier than you think it will.

Grand Marnier
Pastry Cream

2 egg whites (at room
temperature)
2 tablespoons sugar

Preheat your oven to 400°.

Combine Grand Marnier and Pastry Cream into a nice soft foldable mixture (it should not be soupy). You want ¼ cup of this soufflé base.

Beat the egg whites, and, as they begin to rise, add the sugar, a bit at a time, to make a soft-peak meringue.

Fold the soufflé base into the meringue, then scrape into a buttered and sugared individual soufflé dish, as described above.

Bake at 400° for 8-10 minutes.

FRUIT TORTE AU GRAND MARNIER (D.C.)

Makes 3 cakes

Here is a cake made mostly of "leftovers." It uses Pastry Cream (which you may have left over from Coconut Mousse Bombe), Sponge Cake (which you could have left over from Marzipan Bombe); and Grand Marnier liqueur (we always have a leftover bottle of Grand Marnier in our closet).

This recipe will make three cakes, but it can be reduced for just one by dividing everything by three.

The fresh fruits used to top the torte the last time I saw it at the Jockey Club were kiwi fruit, strawberries, fresh raspberries, and bananas.

FILLING:

¾ ounce gelatin
   (3 packets)
¾ cup Grand Marnier
1 pint Pastry Cream, at
   room temperature
   (see page 202)

4 egg whites
¼ cup sugar
1 pint heavy cream

CAKE:

3 ten-inch Sponge Cakes
   (see page 179)
2 tablespoons sugar

3 tablespoons hot water
additional ¼ cup
   Grand Marnier

COOKIE BASE:

1 cup sugar
1 pound sweet butter
1 egg
½ tablespoon vanilla
   extract

½ tablespoon almond
   extract
1½ pounds cake flour
butter for pans

1 cup raspberry jam
fresh fruits
¾ cup apricot
   preserves (for glaze)

¼ cup water
2 tablespoons sugar

The Filling: Soak the gelatin in ¾ cup Grand Marnier and allow it to stand for 10 minutes. Then dissolve the gelatin by heating it gently. Mix it into the Pastry Cream.

Whip the egg whites; as they foam, gradually add ¼ cup of sugar and beat into a soft-peaked meringue. Fold the meringue into the

Pastry Cream mixture.

Whip a pint of heavy cream to soft-peak, and fold that in. Put this filling aside.

Constructing the Torte (Day One): Slice each Sponge Cake into three ½" layers.

(I'll describe the construction of only one Torte.)

Put one layer into the bottom of a 10" cake pan.

Dissolve 2 tablespoons of sugar in 3 tablespoons of hot water, and add ¼ cup Grand Marnier. Take a pastry brush, wet it in this syrup, and dab the surface of the Sponge Cake. You don't want the cake to get soggy, but you do want it well flavored.

After the Sponge Cake layer is flavored, put in about a ½" of the filling. Put another layer of Sponge Cake over the filling, dab with the liqueured brush; repeat with more filling and a third layer. Dab this layer, cover with plastic wrap, and store in the refrigerator overnight.

Cookie Base: Preheat your oven to 375°.

Cream together 1 cup of sugar and 1 pound of butter.

Mix in the egg and the extracts.

Sift and mix in the flour. Do not overmix or it will make one tough cookie!

Butter three 10" cake pans and spoon cookie dough into the bottom of each pan, spreading it evenly, ¼" thick.

Bake in a preheated oven at 375° until lightly colored—about 10 minutes. The cookies can be browned around the edges. Turn them out.

The next day, spread a thin layer of raspberry jam over each cookie, and set them aside.

Constructing the Torte (Day Two): Take the cake pan containing the torte out of the fridge. Dip the pan into hot water up to the rim to loosen the torte. Wipe the pan dry. Place 1 cookie, *jam side down,* onto the Sponge Cake (which is still in the cake pan). Put a 10" cake cardboard on top of the Cookie Base. Now, turn the whole thing over and unmold.

Place slices of fresh fruit on top in concentric circles.

Make an apricot glaze by combining ¾ cup of good quality apricot preserves with ¼ cup of hot water and 2 tablespoons of sugar, and cooking slowly for 10-15 minutes. Strain through a fine strainer, and brush on the fruit very hot.

Each cake serves 14.

■ ████████GÂTEAU GRAND MARNIER (D.C.) ████████ ■

Makes 1 cake, yielding 12 portions

In the Jockey Club kitchen, Marzipan is made with fondant and 2 to 3 cups of powdered sugar, and this is how I have presented this recipe. (In my home kitchen, I make it with simple syrup instead of fondant, and only about 1 cup of powdered sugar. Simple syrup is, simply, sugar dissolved in hot water, in a 2:3 proportion. For approximately ¼ cup syrup, mix together 2 tablespoons of sugar and 3 tablespoons of hot tap water. Using this ¼ cup of simple syrup and 1 cup of powdered sugar, my Marzipan may not be quite as sweet as the Jockey Club's, but Floss and I love it.)

I bought the almond paste necessary for making Marzipan at the best bakery in my neighborhood.

Extra Marzipan—and there is always extra Marzipan after shaping it around the cake—can be stored for another cake, or you can make candy from it: I roll the Marzipan into ½" rods, then cut it into 1" pieces, and dip the pieces into melted chocolate (see the recipe for Chocolate-Dipped Strawberries, page 220).

Chef Danny says that the secret of working with Marzipan is to clean up your act: clean surfaces, clean tools, clean hands, so there are no specks in the Marzipan when rolled.

In my kitchen, I knead the Marzipan on a marble slab saved from our bread-baking days—and feel right at home.

BUTTERCREAM:
1 whole egg
2 egg yolks
water
2 cups sugar

½ pound sweet butter,
   softened
¼ cup (or more) Grand
   Marnier

CAKE:
1 Sponge Cake (see
   page 179)

¼ cup Grand Marnier
¼ cup simple syrup

MARZIPAN COVERING:
1 pound almond paste
4 ounces fondant
red food coloring

2-3 cups confectioners
   sugar

crystallized violets
   (optional, for
   decoration)

Buttercream: Start the Buttercream by mixing together an egg and 2 egg yolks in a mixing bowl; reserve.

In a pot with a cover, add enough water to 2 cups of sugar to make the sugar the consistency of wet sand. Put up to boil, covered; then remove the cover after a few minutes of boiling. Cook to "soft-ball" stage (250° F.)

Begin to beat the eggs a few minutes before the sugar is ready; and when the sugar reaches soft-ball, drizzle it into the eggs—while beating at high speed. Continue to beat the mixture until it is cool (probably about 10 minutes).

Add ½ pound of soft butter, and whip until the texture becomes light.

Flavor to taste, but heavily, with Grand Marnier—don't even bother tasting until you've got a ¼ cup in.

Sponge Cake: Slice the Sponge Cake into three ½" layers.

Mix together the ¼ cup Grand Marnier and the simple syrup.

Set the first layer on a 10" cake cardboard. Moisten the layer with a pastry brush dipped into the syrup/Grand Marnier mixture.

With a spatula, lay on a ½" layer of Buttercream. Then put on another layer of Sponge Cake, and dampen it with the syrup/Grand Marnier mixture. Another ½" layer of Buttercream, and then the last layer of Sponge Cake—and dampen that. Finally, cover the entire cake with Buttercream, and put it in the fridge until the Buttercream hardens.

Making Marzipan: Marzipan is made by mixing together almond paste and a sweetener, and then kneading in confectioners sugar to make it workable. That's right, confectioners sugar is used as flour is used on the kneading board and rolling pin and hands in bread-making.

Lay the almond paste on your kneading surface, and add some fondant (or a small amount of simple syrup) and a tiny bit of red food coloring. Work it in until smooth, and even-colored. Keep adding fondant (or syrup) a little bit at a time, until it feels soft but still cohesive.

Sprinkle confectioners sugar over the board, your hands, the Marzipan, and your rolling pin.

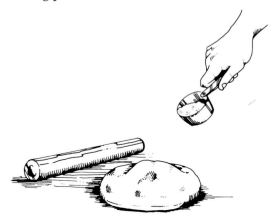

To flatten the Marzipan, powder your hand, and hammer with the heel of your hand in an outward spiral, starting at the center.

Then begin to roll it with the sugared rolling pin. Roll north to south, then east to west, then at diagonals. Keep powdering and turning between rolls. If there is a tear, just press the edges together.

Be generous with the confectioners sugar—it's what makes the Marzipan workable. (There will be sugar left on the surface of the Marzipan even after you get it on the cake. Don't worry: Just brush it off with a soft brush.)

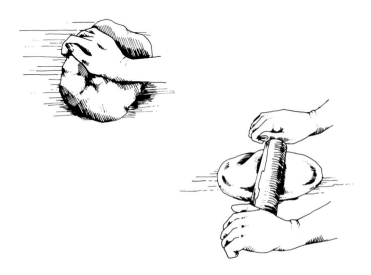

Roll until quite thin, 1/16" or so. You may have to practice a bit until you get it right: It must be thin enough to be shaped to cover the cake, but thick enough to handle.

When you think you have it thin enough, you will pick it up by rolling it onto your rolling pin. Powder the surface of the Marzipan and your pin; lay the pin at one edge of the Marzipan sheet; lift the edge of the sheet with a spatula and hold it lightly against the pin; now, roll the Marzipan around your rolling pin (it will go around the pin a couple of times).

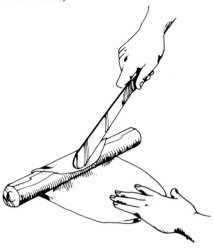

Move your pin to the cold cake, and reverse the rolling. Place the edge of the Marzipan below the bottom of the cake, and unroll, allowing the Marzipan sheet to cover the cake.

When you have the Marzipan sheet over the cake, work out any air pockets, then begin to shape it: *Gently*, poke and prod to make it fit. Again, tears can be just pressed together.

When the Marzipan is shaped to the cake, cut off the excess (about ¼ pound or so) with a sharp knife.

To make the design shown in the photo (see page 176), take a single-edged razor and make a cut through the center of the Marzipan, drawing a line about 4" long, about 3" from each edge, north to south.

Make a similar cut, east to west, and then cut each quarter into thirds. All this cutting will give you 12 wedges of Marzipan, attached to the main body of the Sponge Cake, and show you where the 12 slices go. Lift each flap of Marzipan, and curl it back, as shown in the photo.

Optionally, you can decorate each slice on the cake with a rosette of Buttercream and a crystallized violet.

MARZIPAN BOMBE (D.C.)

Serves plenty

Here is another beautiful "construction." The "Sauce Melba" called for is a commercial raspberry sauce, sometimes found masquerading as an ice-cream topping. "Raspberry reduction" is concentrated raspberries: 3 cups of raw raspberries cooked over low heat to a ½ cup. Make it ahead of time and cool it in your refrigerator.

CHOCOLATE WHIPPED CREAM:

12 ounces semisweet chocolate, melted, cooled to 100°

1 pint heavy cream

RASPBERRY WHIPPED CREAM:

1 pint heavy cream
½ cup raspberry reduction

¼ cup Sauce Melba

GRAND MARNIER WHIPPED CREAM:

1 pint heavy cream
1-2 ounces Grand Marnier (to taste)

1 cup fresh raspberries (or strawberries)

SYRUP:

½ cup simple syrup (4 tablespoons sugar/ 6 tablespoons hot water)

½ cup Kirschwasser
½ cup Grand Marnier

CAKE:

1 Sponge Cake (see page 179)

2 Chocolate Sponge Cakes (see page 192)

MARZIPAN:

2 pounds almond paste
½ pound fondant

about 5 cups confectioners sugar

Making the Whipped Creams: Chocolate—Melt the chocolate, then allow it to cool until it is barely warm on your lip; whip the cream quite soft (just before soft-peak); pour all the chocolate into the whipped cream, then whip like the very devil for 2 or 3 seconds only, and stop. Fold gently to finish blending (over-beating will cause the cream to break).

Raspberry—Whip the cream to soft-peak; fold in the cool raspberry reduction and the Sauce Melba.

Grand Marnier—Whip the cream to soft-peak and fold in the Grand Marnier, tasting after the first ounce is in; fold in the berries.

Syrup: Dissolve 4 tablespoons of sugar in 6 tablespoons of hot water. Add ½ cup each of Kirschwasser and Grand Marnier, and stir.

Assembling the Bombe: Slice each Sponge Cake into three ½" layers.

As the bombe is assembled, every layer of sponge will be moistened by being dabbed with a pastry brush dipped repeatedly into the syrup.

I'll describe the making of one bombe.

Line the inside of an 8½" bombe mold with plastic wrap.

Cut a 4" disk from a layer of plain Sponge Cake, set it in the bottom of the mold, and press it into place. (Please note that you can cut *two* 4" disks from a single layer—one for each bombe.) Moisten it well with a pastry brush dipped into the syrup. (Each layer of cake should be damp, but not soggy.)

Spoon in and spread a layer of Raspberry Whipped Cream, 1" thick.

Cut a layer of Chocolate Sponge Cake to fit the bowl (about 6"), and set it on top of the filling. Moisten it with Syrup.

Spread a layer of the Grand Marnier Whipped Cream with berries, about 1" thick.

Cut a layer of plain Sponge Cake to fit the bowl (about 7"), set it on top of the filling, and moisten it with the Syrup.

Now spread a 1" layer of Chocolate Whipped Cream.

Put on the final layer (8½") of Chocolate Sponge Cake, and moisten it with syrup.

Repeat for the second bombe.

Cover both molds with plastic wrap and refrigerate overnight.

Next day, make the Marzipan, as instructed in Gâteau Grand Marnier (recipe on page 208). Divide the Marzipan in half and roll out one of the pieces.

When your sheet of Marzipan is thin enough (quite thin, but not falling apart), and large enough to fit over the whole bombe, roll it onto the rolling pin by placing the pin at one edge, and helping it with your hands or a steel spatula. You want all the Marzipan sheet rolled onto the pin.

Remove the bombe from the refrigerator. Unmold it by inverting it onto a cake cardboard or a cake plate. Remove the plastic wrap.

Put your rolling pin next to the bombe and unroll the Marzipan over the bombe. Gently, shape the Marzipan to the dome with your fingers, then cut away the excess at the bottom. Repeat for the second bombe.

■ ■■■■■■■RASPBERRY MOUSSE (D.C.)■■■■■■ ■

Yields about 16 four-ounce servings

This is a raspberry lover's dream. And very easy to make. The raspberry reduction is made of 6 pints of raspberries (overripe and soft raspberries are fine for this) cooked over low heat until they are 1 pint. It is not sweet. The Sauce Melba is a commercial product, available in some gourmet shops and sometimes where ice-cream toppings are sold. I have made the recipe without it, and it comes out a little paler, but just as delicious. Framboise is a raspberry brandy, colorless, and very strong-flavored, but also not sweet.

1 pint raspberry **reduction**	**2 ounces Framboise**
1 packet gelatin	**12 egg whites**
½ cup cold water	**3 cups sugar**
1 quart heavy cream	**½ cup Sauce Melba**

Allow the raspberry reduction to cool to room temperature.

Combine the gelatin and water. Allow to stand for about 10 minutes, then heat gently to dissolve the gelatin. Allow to cool slightly, while still remaining liquid.

Meanwhile, whip the cream and Framboise together until soft-peak. Put aside.

Begin whipping the egg whites; as they begin to foam, add the sugar bit by bit. Whip to soft-peak.

Combine the raspberry reduction, the Sauce Melba, and the gelatin, mixing well.

Fold the raspberry mixture into the egg whites.

Fold the whipped cream into the raspberry mix.

Refrigerate.

■ ■■BLACK FOREST KIRSCH TORTE (D.C.)■■ ■
Black Forest Cherry Cake

This torte makes 12 servings

Here is a traditional chocolate torte, flavored with Kirschwasser—cherry brandy. The cherries called for are canned, pitted black bing cherries. It is important that the cherries be sweet and flavorful.

In this recipe, a pastry bag is used to lay down the whipped cream. If you've never used a pastry bag, see page 224 for some instruction. Squeezing the cream out of the bag this way is called "piping," and the circles we make are called "concentric pipe rings."

CAKE:
1 ten-inch Chocolate Sponge
Cake (see page 192)

SYRUP:
2 ounces sugar dissolved   **¼ cup Kirschwasser**
in 3 ounces hot water

FILLING:
12 ounces semisweet   **2 cups (or more) canned**
chocolate   **black cherries, drained**
1 pint heavy cream

COVERING:
1 pint heavy cream   **4 tablespoons**
2 ounces Kirschwasser   **confectioner's sugar**

DECORATION:
12 cherries   **dry Chocolate Sponge**
shavings of semisweet   **Cake crumbs (optional)**
chocolate, for finishing

Slice the Sponge Cake into three ½" layers. Place one layer on a cake cardboard or cake plate.

Make the Syrup by combining the sugar and hot water, and then mixing in the Kirschwasser.

Moisten that first layer of sponge with a pastry brush dipped in the Syrup.

Making the Filling: Melt the chocolate in the top of a double boiler and allow it cool back to about 100° (warm on the lip).

Whip a pint of cream to just a bit softer than soft-peak. Pour in all the chocolate, then whip like the devil for 2 or 3 seconds—then stop. Fold in any unmixed chocolate. Do not overmix.

Piping: We are going to make concentric circles of Chocolate Filling and cherries.

Put a large tip into your pastry bag; fill the bag partway; and, beginning at the center, pipe in a small disk of Filling onto the center of the cake. (This first bit of Filling will be about 4" across and about as high as a cherry.)

Place a circle of touching cherries, all the way around this disk of Filling.

Around the cherries, pipe in a circle of Filling, about ¾" thick.

Do another circle of cherries, and end the layer with a final circle of Filling.

Place a layer of Sponge Cake on top of this one you've just filled, and moisten it with the Syrup.

With a spatula, spread a ½" thickness of the Chocolate Whipped Cream over the entire top of this layer.

Place the last layer of Sponge Cake on top, and moisten it with Syrup.

Make the Covering: Whip a pint of heavy cream until it thickens but doesn't yet hold shape. Add 2 ounces of Kirsch and 4 tablespoons of powdered sugar, and whip until stiff-peak.

Cover the top and sides of the cake.

Decorate the top of the torte with a circle of 12 rosettes (one for each serving) near the edge. Make the rosettes from the Kirsch-and-whipped-cream covering, squeezed from a small pastry bag with a serrated medium tip. Place a cherry in the center of each rosette. Sprinkle semisweet chocolate shavings over the top and sides.

If you have them, decorate the side of the cake with some dry chocolate cake crumbs touched to the bottom inch.

■ ■■■ CHOCOLATE TRUFFLE TORTE (D.C.) ■■■ ■

Yields 3 tortes

Here is an unbelievably chocolate-rich cake. Please note that the cake in this recipe is not sponge cake but good-old-raised-by-baking-powder cake. The recipe makes three 10" tortes of 3 layers each. Yes, there are 2 batches of Ganache called for.

Make sure that all the refrigerated ingredients are at room temperature before mixing them in.

To keep the batter smooth throughout, scrape down the bowl and beaters between each addition.

DARK CAKE:
1½ cups sugar
1½ cups dark-brown
  sugar
7 ounces sweet butter
1⅓ cups cocoa powder,
  sifted
2 ounces unsweetened
  chocolate
5 large eggs (at room
  temperature)

1⅝ cups buttermilk
  (at room temperature)
6 cups cake flour
  (measured after sifting)
1 tablespoon baking soda
1½ cups water
  (at room temperature)
butter (for pans)
flour (for pans)

GANACHE #1 (Filling):
2 pounds semisweet
  chocolate

3 cups heavy cream

GANACHE #2 (Topping):
1 pound semisweet
  chocolate

1½ cups heavy cream

TRUFFLES:
1 pound semisweet
  chocolate

additional chocolate
  (for grating)

Making the Cake: Preheat your oven to about 360°.

Mix together until creamy the sugar, brown sugar, butter, and sifted cocoa powder.

Melt 2 ounces of unsweetened chocolate, and mix in well.

Mixing well, one at a time, add the eggs.

Add a little of the buttermilk.

Sift together the cake flour and baking soda, and mix in some of that.

Alternate mixing in the buttermilk and flour, keeping the batter smooth.

Mix in the tap water (at room temperature, remember), and make a smooth batter.

Rub the insides of three 10″ cake pans with butter, and flour lightly.

Divide the batter among the pans, and bake at 360° for about 30 minutes, until a cake tester (or a clean straw) comes out with no batter sticking to it.

Cool 20 minutes in the pan, then turn out onto a rack and cool completely.

When cool, cut each cake into 3 equal layers, place each bottom layer on a 10″ cake cardboard, and assemble the tortes on racks. (The racks should be over trays to catch the extra topping as it drips down.)

The Filling: Chop 2 pounds of semisweet chocolate into small bits. Meanwhile, put 3 cups of heavy cream up to boil.

Put the chocolate into a mixing bowl, and pour the hot cream over it, and stir (don't beat) until uniform. This is Ganache #1.

Allow the Ganache to cool until it is as thick as soft butter.

Whip it by machine for a few seconds only, until it turns lighter in color. Do not overwhip or it will break.

Spread the Ganache ¼" thick as a filling between the layers, and in a thin coating over the entire outside of the cake.

Refrigerate the remaining Ganache for several hours. When completely firmed we will use it to make the Truffles.

The Topping: Make up Ganache #2 in the same way.

Allow it to cool a bit (but not really to thicken).

Pour this Ganache over the 3 tortes. The excess will drip down through the rack into the tray below. It can be scraped up and reused or saved.

The Truffles: Remove the now-firm bowl of Ganache #1 from the fridge.

Using a melon baller dipped repeatedly in hot water, cut 36 balls out of the cold Ganache, and put them aside.

Meanwhile, in the top of a double boiler, gently melt a pound of semisweet chocolate.

Grate some additional semisweet chocolate through the coarsest holes of your kitchen grater, onto some baker's parchment on a flat surface.

Dip the Ganache balls into the hot chocolate, then roll them in the chocolate shavings. Set the balls aside and let the chocolate harden.

Place 12 Truffles around the top of each cake, near the rim, to mark the 12 helpings. Use a dot of Ganache #2 to hold each Truffle in place.

▪ PETITS FOURS ▪

Like so many colloquial phrases, it's hard to pin down the exact derivation of *petits fours*. Literally, it means "little ovens." Certainly, the pieces themselves are usually small. Perhaps the reference is to the small amount of baking (or cooking) time required.

At the New York Jockey Club, a selection of petits fours is served after the meal—or after dessert.

CHOCOLATE-DIPPED STRAWBERRIES

Yields about 50 large berries

These, of course, should be prepared on the day they are to be eaten. If there are any left after the party, eat them yourself.

These are so easy to make, and yet they elicit more admiration than much more complicated dishes. Ah, well, who said a chef's life was an easy one.

The flavor of the chocolate makes the flavor of the dish. A rich chocolate makes a rich taste. Floss and I have found no supermarket chocolate to be adequate. Lately, we have been buying chocolate in 10-pound bars from a local candymaker, and hacking off as much as we need for a recipe, then wrapping the balance in plastic and storing it in our cool (but not frigid) basement. A few minutes spent with the Yellow Pages were quite worthwhile.

½ **pound semisweet chocolate**	**1 quart ripe strawberries**

In the top of a small double boiler, over moderate heat, melt the chocolate, and then allow it to cool somewhat. The chocolate should be hot enough to be fluid, but cool enough to allow you to dip a finger without any discomfort.

Do not wash the berries. If you must wash them, allow them to be *completely* dry before you dip them. However, do pick over the strawberries and remove any that are underripe—or rotten or wounded (you don't want the juice to mix into the chocolate).

Place a large piece of baker's parchment (or aluminum foil) on a baking tray.

To dip, pick up a berry by its leaves and lower it up to its "shoulder" (the place at the top where it curves in) in the melted chocolate. Don't let go.

Pull out, allow to drip for a few seconds, and then brush off the excess chocolate by gently scraping one side of the berry against an inside edge of the chocolate pot.

Place the berry on the parchment, allowing it to lean on the place where you scraped off the chocolate. This allows the chocolate to look smooth and unbroken.

Repeat for every berry.

A ½ pound of chocolate should be enough for about 50 berries—about a quart.

For best display, use berries that are more or less uniform in size.

■ ■━━━━━━■CHOCOLATE-DIPPED■━━━━━■ ■
MACADAMIA NUTS

A cluster of 3 macadamia nuts makes 1 piece

The nuts should be lightly roasted in a moderate oven and allowed to cool before dipping.

Melt the chocolate and allow it to cool, as you did with Chocolate-Dipped Strawberries (see page 220).

Drop a nut into the chocolate, dip it out with a fork, allow it to drip for a few seconds, then place on parchment or foil. Add a second dipped nut, touching, and then a third dipped nut to complete the triangle. Continue until you are out of nuts, chocolate, or patience.

I warn you: Though these require a lot more time to make than Chocolate-Dipped Strawberries, your guests will not be nearly as impressed.

If you can't find macadamias in sufficient quantity for your needs, the Jockey Club has been known to substitute lightly roasted hazelnuts in this recipe.

Tiles

Yields 40 large cookies

Tuiles means "tiles"—and this time the derivation is quite clear: These cookies are shaped to look like the rounded roof tiles you see in France. I have reduced the recipe to yield about 40 cookies (the one I began with started out "20 eggs . . .").

The hot Tuiles will have to be scraped off the baking sheets. A clean wide putty knife works very well—especially if you don't have a very stiff and wide spatula.

A 2″ paint brush (used exclusively as a pastry brush, please) works well and quickly to butter the trays.

3 eggs	**½ cup flour**
5 ounces almonds, sliced	**melted sweet butter (for**
and blanched	**the trays)**
1 cup sugar	

Preheat your oven to 400°.

Beat together the eggs, almonds, and sugar.

Add the flour and mix well.

Lightly brush melted butter on several cookie sheets. A large sheet will hold 9 cookies, a small sheet only 6. In my kitchen, I washed and rebuttered the baking sheets as they came out and the cookies were scraped off and shaped.

Drop teaspoon-sized lumps of batter onto a sheet, well separated. These cookies will really spread.

Take a cup of hot water, dip a fork in it, and mash the cookie batter on the baking sheet until they are quite thin. Repeat for all the cookies, for as many trays as your oven will hold.

Bake for about 6 minutes, until the cookies have turned brown only around the edges.

Shaping the Tuiles: Tuiles are shaped immediately after baking. If you have a mold (it looks like several narrow U-shaped gutters held together), then simply place the cookies into the mold as you scrape them off the sheets.

If you have no mold, the cookies can be shaped over a 1″ thick wooden dowel or a clean metal pipe or a broomstick. I use a broomstick with a clean towel over the handle, placed over a sink so the cookies can hang.

Scrape a cookie off the pan and place it over the broomstick or into the mold. Keep scraping as long as the cookies come off readily. If they begin to cool, they will have to be put back into the oven for a minute (only!). This warming softens them again, and makes them easy to remove from the tray.

After only a couple of minutes on the broom, they are cooled enough to keep their shape, and the first on can be taken off to make room for the later-comers.

This recipe yields about 40 large, though thin, cookies.

If you need more than that, write to me and I will send you the original—it will yield about 280.

LANGUES DE CHAT
Cat's Tongues

Yields dozens of cookies

The literal translation for this delicious butter cookie is an appetizing "cat's tongues." To make them you will have to use a pastry bag —and if you never have, there are a few hints for handling a pastry bag below.

6 tablespoons sweet butter, softened	**2 egg whites**
⅔ cup confectioners sugar	**⅔ cup flour**

Preheat your oven to 400°.

Spread the butter in a bowl and sprinkle over it the sugar and egg whites, and blend together.

Add and mix in the flour.

When the mixture is quite smooth, scrape it into a pastry bag with a ¼″ serrated tip.

Lay a sheet of baker's parchment over a large cookie sheet.

Squeeze out elongated "cat's tongues," about 1½″ long and ¼″ wide. Allow them space to spread about double or triple, but do get as many as you can on the sheet: This recipe fills a large cookie sheet.

The finished cookie will be grooved, and its shape will be an elongated and flattened lozenge.

Bake at 400° for about 6 minutes, but be prepared to rotate the trays after 4 or 5 minutes. (Few ovens bake evenly enough.)

Using a Pastry Bag

We use a pastry bag in the making of Langues de Chat, Concord Cake (page 184), Black Forest Kirsch Torte (page 216), Gâteau Marjolaine (page 200), and others. It's a good skill to have.

A pastry bag is a canvas or coated cloth, stitched into a cone shape, wide open at one end and with a narrow opening at the other.

A metal tip is fitted (just by being snug, on most) into the narrow end of the bag by pushing it through from the wide end. It is this tip that determines whether you'll get a lot of batter or a little, and whether that batter is to be plain or decorated. The serrated tip used in the recipe for Langues de Chat cuts into the batter as it is squeezed out. That design is then kept as the cookie bakes, giving it its striped look.

After the appropriate tip is in place (small and serrated for this recipe, but plain and large for Concord Cake), the batter is scraped into the bag. But, first, fold the bag back so that about the top third is over your spread thumb and forefinger. This will hold the top widespread for loading.

Don't fill the bag more than halfway. If it's a large recipe, the bag may have to be refilled.

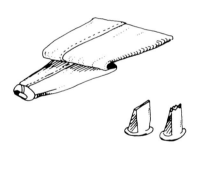

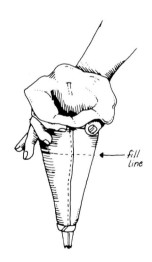

fill line

Once some batter is in, hold the bag over the bowl in which you mixed the batter, and twist the bag closed. That twist should be just at the level of the batter. The twist closes off the top of the bag and prevents batter from backing up on you.

The twist of the bag is held between the thumb and forefinger of your stronger hand. Your fingers on that hand press the bag to force the batter out. The tips of the index and forefinger of your other hand are used to direct the tip. Use only the very tips—this gives you the clearest view of your work.

When the bag empties somewhat, retwist, but always keep the bag over the bowl when you do—or you may find batter on your toes.

If you have to put the bag down before the job is finished, put it down on a clean surface, not into the bowl. The outside of the bag can get quite dirty.

When you are finished, remove the tip, rinse it out, and wash and dry. Rinse the bag to get rid of the batter, and then throw it into the washing machine. With most, no special treatment is demanded.

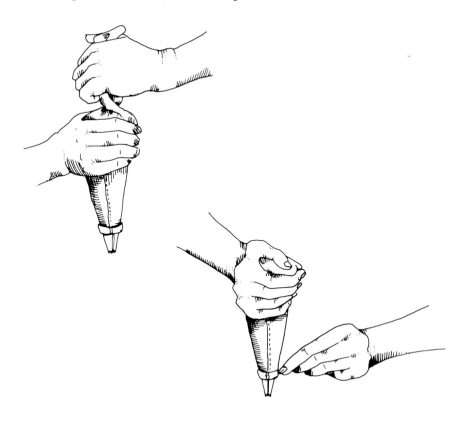

Yields dozens of pieces, depending on the size you cut them

This is a treat made of a combination of almonds and glazed cherries in a sweet and creamy filling, over a cookie crust. The finished pastry is so sweet that it is cut into small pieces for serving. We found a pizza wheel just right for cutting most of the way, then a knife for finishing the job.

The glucose called for in the Filling is available in the supermarket, but I found it convenient to substitute honey.

PASTRY CRUST:
1 pound sweet butter
1 generous cup sugar
3 eggs
⅜ cup heavy cream
1 teaspoon salt

½ tablespoon vanilla
  extract
1¾ pounds flour
  (about 7 cups)

FILLING:
1¼ cups heavy cream
2 sticks plus 1
  tablespoon sweet
  butter
8 ounces honey
1 pound sugar

4 ounces glucose
1 pound 10 ounces
  almonds, sliced and
  blanched
1 pound 2 ounces glazed
  cherries

Preheat your oven to 400°.

Combine all the crust ingredients (except the flour), and mix until quite smooth.

Add the flour and just mix until it becomes uniform—do not overwork.

Roll it out on a large buttered baking sheet (the dough need not go up the sides of the sheet), then put it into the freezer until you've made the filling.

Combine all the Filling ingredients except the nuts and cherries in a pan, and cook over medium-high heat for about 5 minutes after it comes to a boil, stirring occasionally.

Remove from heat, and stir in the almonds and cherries very well.

Take another baking sheet and scrape the mixture onto it, using a spatula to spread it evenly over the bottom. Put it into the oven to bake at 400° for about 20 minutes, or until it has become a light brown. After 10 or 15 minutes, pull the rack out of the oven and stir until the browning parts are well mixed in.

When the top is light brown (after a total of about 20 minutes), remove from the oven and stir all this stuff again.

Remove the crust from the freezer and scrape the filling onto it, again leveling everything with a spatula.

Return to the oven and bake again at 400°, for about a ½ hour, until the top is a more-or-less uniform medium brown. Remove from the oven when done, allow to rest for about 20 minutes, and then cut into ½" by 1" or so pieces.

■ PART FIVE ■

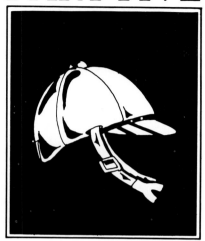

■ INDEX ■

INDEX

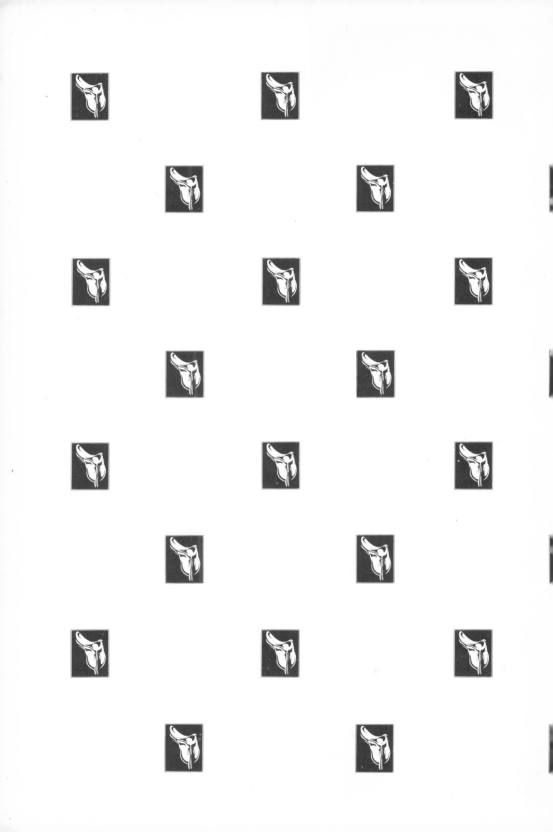